CANADIAN WAR HEROES

Ten Profiles in Courage

11/05

-2

Giancarlo La Giorgia

FOLK
LORE
PUBLISHING

The Publisher: Folklore Publishing

Website: www.folklorepublishing.com

Library and Archives Canada Cataloguing in Publication

La Giorgia, Giancarlo, 1980–
  Canadian war heroes : ten profiles in courage / Giancarlo
  La Giorgia.

(Great Canadian stories)
ISBN 1-894864-35-2

    1. Canada—Biography. 2. Heroes—Canada—Biography. 3.
Canada—History, Military. I. Title. II. Series.

FC25.L33 2005   355'.00921'271   C2005-900637-4

Project Director: Faye Boer
Project Editor: Terry McIntyre
Production: Linda Bolger, Trina Koscielnuk
Cover Image: Courtesy of National Archives of Canada, PA-1654

We acknowledge the support of the Alberta Foundation for the Arts for our publishing program.

PC:P6

Table of Contents

Dedication

To my *bebek*, Rita,
all the inspiration I'll ever need.

Acknowledgements

SINCEREST THANKS TO LINDA KAY, for introducing me to Folklore Publishing, and for being the first to believe I could actually write this book. To publisher Faye Boer, for giving me my first big break, as well as two months of my life that I likely won't ever forget. To both Concordia University librarian Sonia Poulin, and the staff of the Eleanor London Library, for helping me to navigate the dusty shelves of Canadian history. To Princess Patricia's Canadian Light Infantry (PPCLI) Lieutenant-Colonel Schreiber, Major Ted Giraldeau and Lieutenant Peebles for their invaluable help. To my friends—Jon, Julia, Shirley, Maurice, Louis, Billy and Matt—as well as my ex-professor, Denise Roig. Your encouragement was much appreciated. To my family, including the Pehlivanians, for supporting me when I was unsupportable—no one said having a writer in the family would be easy. Most of all, to my sweet little Rita, soon-to-be Mrs. La Giorgia. Only you would take on the thankless task of dealing with my self-doubt, mood swings, and the growth in beard and belly that only self-imposed exile can bring. But don't worry babe, I'm sure you'll get used to it. Love ya.

Introduction

See, the conquering hero comes! Sound the trumpets, beat the drums. Sports prepare, the laurel bring, songs of triumph to him sing…See the godlike youth advance! Breathe the flutes, and lead the dance; Myrtle wreaths, and roses twine, to deck the hero's brow divine.

—Georg Friedrich Händel's
Judas Maccabaeus

Canada is a safe, tranquil place filled with friendly, peace-loving people. Or so it seems.

In other, more warlike nations, obscene amounts of money can freely be spent on improving "defence" capabilities, usually with unquestioning enthusiasm from an extremely nationalistic population. Meanwhile, the government spends just enough to buy new mothballs for its antique collection of tanks, helicopters and submarines, usually with subdued sarcasm from an otherwise indifferent Canadian public. True, Canada once boasted the world's third largest navy, fourth largest air force and an army of six divisions, but the brief glory days of our Canadian Forces have now all but faded from collective memory, suiting most Canadians just fine. After all, why maintain a huge, costly fighting force if no one really wants to fight against Canada?

Of course, every country must have the means to defend itself—even the neutral Swiss have their army knives! Yet, for the most part, Canadians feel secure that their (somewhat exaggerated) presence in international peacekeeping and humanitarian efforts will somehow inoculate them against the violence that has infected the rest of the world.

The unfortunate consequence of this quaint naïveté is that Canadians have become a people with little attachment to their military's institutions and history, and even less stomach for the occasionally necessary evil of warfare. Unsurprisingly, there has been an ever-increasing deterioration in the feelings of basic gratitude owed to the generations of Canadian soldiers who made the ultimate sacrifice for their country. Remembrance Day has become Remembrance Minute, while, for a growing number, the sudden bloom of poppies in mid-November stirs little or no sentiment at all. Some might go so far as to reject the very premise of this book, arguing that a person cannot be considered heroic by Canadian standards if they participated in large-scale, government-sanctioned fighting and killing. Yet, whether pacifist, warmonger or somewhere in-between, to disregard Canadian war heroism is tantamount to rejecting the Canadian identity. Welcome it or not, the basic characteristics of Canada's national identity— bilingual, multiracial, free and democratic—owe their evolution, in large part, to the outcome of

every war since the French, English and First
Nations began to cohabit this great land.

I must confess that, before sitting down to write
this book, I myself had a hard time understanding
how someone could willingly risk his or her life
for a concept as abstract as a country. I couldn't
truly appreciate the Armed Forces dedication to
defending Canada, or any other nation—not for
any lack of patriotism, but simply because I have
never felt especially threatened living in "boring
(c)old" Canada. However, as I researched the cast
of characters whose daring exploits fill these pages,
I became aware of two things: times of peace are
rather fleeting (as the recent rash of global terrorism has reminded us) and in times of action,
Canadians are not such a gentle race after all—
especially when being attacked by an invariably
larger, stronger and better-equipped enemy. In
fact, Canadian soldiers have always been counted
as being among the finest warriors around, from
the War of 1812, where Charles de Salaberry and
his ragtag band of 500 Voltigeurs defeated an
American force of 4000 troops through sheer cunning, to the latter days of World War II, when the
Canadian Army as part of the Allied Forces helped
to liberate the people of Holland from Nazi clutches.

This isn't to say that I've become a war booster
by any means. I still agree with the old adage that
"war is hell," frequently mismanaged by incom-
petent leaders, and at times, an utterly pointless
exercise, except in providing brisk business for

undertakers and tombstone makers. But even so, there comes a time when conscientious objection is no longer an option—it is an act of open contempt for this country, which can only stand free as long as all of our fellow countrymen are united against those who would do Canada harm. I now have a better grasp of the vital role that armed conflict has played in shaping this country, and moreover, the outstanding historical figures whose actions have proved decisive.

This book is a collection of profiles exploring the many facets of war heroism and chronicling both lives and deeds of 10 of the most important war heroes in Canadian history. It supplies a good measure of quirks and controversies as well, such as the fact that none of the first four profiles are about people actually born in Canada, or that one of this book's most well-known subjects, ace World War I pilot Billy Bishop, has been accused of (allegedly) having lied about most, if not all, of his 72 victory claims. Then there's the small detail that the last chapter isn't the profile of a single person, but an entire regiment. Each chapter offers a snapshot of the remarkable lives lived and battles fought by these very different Canadian heroes: Sir Isaac Brock, Tecumseh and Laura Secord in the War of 1812; the Marquis de Montcalm in the Seven Years' War; Alexander Roberts Dunn in the Crimean War; William Avery "Billy" Bishop, Sir Arthur Currie and Georges-Philéas Vanier in World War I; Roméo Dallaire in

the UN peacekeeping mission to Rwanda dur-
ing the Rwandan Genocide; and finally, the entire
Princess Patricia's Canadian Light Infantry
Regiment, which has fought in nearly every
important Canadian battle from the Great War up
to the recent NATO strike against the Taliban and
Al-Qaeda forces in Afghanistan, as part of the
War on Terrorism.

I hope that, after reading about these truly inspir-
ing and genuinely interesting characters, a new
respect might be found for the men and women
currently serving in the Canadian Forces. Despite
all adversity and the natural instinct for self-
preservation, they remain committed to defending the country, institutions and way of life—with
their own lives, if necessary. Like most of the
thousands upon thousands of Canadian soldiers
who have fought and died before them, they are
mostly anonymous, and appear as unremarkable
outside of their military garb as do you or I. They
don't ask that huge monuments be erected in
their names or even that there be agreement with
the violence inherent with their trade, just that
there is a bit of gratitude shown for their danger-
ous, underappreciated and unbelievably difficult
work.

That's why, in my book, they're all heroes.

CHAPTER ONE

Sir Isaac Brock
(1769–1812)

August 12, 1812.

AT FORT DETROIT IN MICHIGAN TERRITORY, the Army of the Northwest is preparing to deliver what it hopes will be a fatal blow to the defences of Upper Canada's western front. Brigadier-General William Hull commands the United States' 2200-strong vanguard force, eager to win this first major battle of the War of 1812 and send "John Bull" running back to England.

Across the Detroit River, among the farmhouses of Sandwich Town (present-day Windsor, Ontario) and about 30 kilometres downstream at Fort Malden in Amherstburg, Ontario, the British troops under Major-General Isaac Brock are outnumbered almost two to one, vastly outgunned and overly reliant on fighters of questionable allegiance. With the bulk of her regular soldiers battling for survival against Napoleon's armies in Europe, Britain has had to inject the anemic military of her North American colonies with unwieldy Native warriors and reluctant Canadian-born militiamen. This despite the fact that many among the former group have fought against or been betrayed by the British in the past, while among the latter are many recent American immigrants and some French-Canadians, all of them objects of British suspicion for either secretly wishing or openly conspiring for a U.S. victory.

America has good cause for optimism: her population nears eight million patriotic souls (Canada's population was only 300,000), still buoyed by the Revolutionary War won only a generation earlier, and she boasts 10 times the military power and resources of Canada. Indeed, many are quite convinced that, with the slightest threat, Canada's British regime will topple like a house of cards. The prevailing wisdom, summed up best by U.S. President Thomas Jefferson, was that the acquisition of Canada would be "a mere matter of marching."

However, the Americans ended up surrendering Fort Detroit after a (near) bloodless battle, and Hull, like General Custer after him, became one of the more famous losers in U.S. military history. The would-be conquerors of Canada seem to have underestimated the legendary stubbornness of Canadian soldiers when fighting a battle they weren't supposed to win. Moreover, in all their boastful calculations, the U.S. didn't factor in their opponents' cunning and fearless leader, Isaac Brock. For his conspicuous bravery, he was heralded across the British Empire, posthumously received a knighthood and will be forever known as the "Saviour of Upper Canada."

But how could the fate of Canada have been decided by a man with an avowed hatred of democracy or any form of self-determination, little concept of human rights—he wanted to suspend habeas corpus and force militiamen, regardless of their heritage, to pledge allegiance to (Mad) King George III—and a deep resentment for his appointment to a "colonial backwater" while his comrades fought for glory alongside the Duke of Wellington in Europe?

Simply put, Brock put duty ahead of happiness and the lives of others before his own. He was a hero, one of Canada's first.

Isaac Brock was born on October 6, 1769, in St. Peter Port, Guernsey, one of the Channel Islands off the coast of Normandy, France. He was the eighth son of Elizabeth de Lisle and John Brock, a former midshipman, or sub-lieutenant, in the Royal Navy who died at age 48, when Isaac was only eight years old. In 1779, at age 10, Isaac began his academic life, eventually enrolling at Elizabeth College in Guernsey where, when not practicing Hebrew, Greek, Latin, French, German, Spanish, Italian, drawing, music, fencing and drilling, he was cultivating a reputation as a tremendous athlete, especially in swimming and later boxing. However, at the tender age of 15, despite the recent loss of his brother Ferdinand, who died at 19 while serving in Bâton Rouge, Louisiana, Isaac decided he was not cut out for

academic life and purchased a commission in the
8th (King's) Regiment, where another brother,
John, was a captain.

By age 22, Isaac had grown considerably in both
rank and stature. He was then a captain in the
49th Regiment of Foot, stationed from 1791–93 in
Barbados and Jamaica, and was already, in his
own words, "as tough as nails." By most accounts,
he was a handsome man with a fair complexion,
broad forehead, sparkling white teeth and
almond-shaped, grey-blue eyes—one with a
slight, permanent squint. He measured about
1.9 metres (6'3") in height, had a broad frame and
an athletic physique, attributes that went a long
way toward commanding both the fear and
respect of those who met him. Respect, however,
was apparently not something Isaac ever seemed
to lack from either superiors or subordinates.
Although he advocated the strongest punishment
for disobedient soldiers and was occasionally
faulted by higher-ranking officers for his impul-
siveness, his troops loved him for his fairness, his
leadership by example and his concern for their
well-being. In later years, the stone-faced general
was fondly remembered by his troops for petition-
ing Canada's governor general to grant Crown
land to retired veterans as repayment for their
services, for being the first to jump into the cold
waters of Lake Erie when a boat in which he was
travelling became stuck on a rock and for shed-
ding a tear at the execution of a mutinous soldier.

Even the few detractors among his superiors couldn't deny that his style of fearless offence tended to cow opponents into submission.

One such colourful example took place during his time in the Caribbean. At Bridgetown, Barbados, there was a most ungentlemanly officer and accomplished gunfighter who got his kicks from insulting fellow officers, challenging them to a duel and finishing them off at a dozen paces. When this hooligan marked Captain Brock as his next victim, he duly consented to a showdown. However, the morning of the showdown, when the smirking duellist asked sardonically, "How many paces would you like to take before you die?" Brock delivered a challenge of his own. He brandished a handkerchief from his breast pocket and, holding it from one corner, extended it to his adversary with the humourless reply, "Hold the other end." Unwilling to fire at point-blank range and risk his own life, the disgraced coward slunk off the battlefield and soon withdrew entirely from the military.

But, for all Brock's plucky courage, he would only have two opportunities to prove his mettle on the battlefield prior to his arrival in Canada. In 1799, at age 30, after 15 years of service, after climbing the ranks to senior lieutenant-colonel, he finally saw action in Britain's victorious Battle of Egmont-op-zee, in French-allied Holland. He was accompanied by his 16-year-old brother Savery, a burly, headstrong youth who rivalled his older sibling in daring and over whom Isaac was rather protective, as well as Lieutenant-Colonel Roger Sheaffe, who would one day fight alongside the elder Brock in North America. Here, the 49th suffered relatively high losses, and Isaac himself was nearly killed by a musket ball to the neck, the force of which was sufficient to knock him clear off his horse. Once again, he was saved by a handkerchief, which he wrapped around a thick silk cravat he was wearing on account of cold weather, and after regaining his bearings, he continued to fight. Young Savery also distinguished himself that day by putting himself in the line of fire to rally his fellow soldiers at the expense of a severe scolding from his big brother.

Two years later, in 1801, Brock and his regiment were onboard one of the gun ships sailing for battle with Denmark. They expected to take part in a land assault on heavily fortified Copenhagen, but Britain's incredible naval victory there, owing in large part to the legendary Horatio Nelson, made the invasion unnecessary. Nevertheless, Brock was fortunate enough to take note of Nelson's audacity and tactical brilliance, as well as his creative disregard of orders. (At a point when the British were close to losing, Admiral Sir Hyde Parker signalled Nelson to end the fighting and pull back. Nelson, cleverly, decided to disobey. Having lost his right eye in a previous battle, he turned to his ship's captain and said, "I only have one eye, I have a right to be blind," and, with the telescope on his sightless eye, exclaimed, "I really do not see the signal.")

Finally, in 1802, Brock, the men of the 49th and their families were requisitioned to Québec City. During the decade leading up to the War of 1812, his troops were transported back and forth between the military posts of Upper and Lower Canada, while Brock himself was forced to shuttle between his steadily increasing military and civil responsibilities.

By 1811, Brock was both a major-general and the chief administrator of Upper Canada, a fitting pair of titles for such a firm believer in autocratic rule and perhaps a consolation for having to endure life in the muddy little capital of York (Toronto), far away from family, friends and the fighting in Europe. As a politician blessed with a military mind, Brock began preparing for war with the U.S. as far back as 1807, when he compelled the dovish Governor General George Prevost to restore Québec's dilapidated fortress to its former glory.

Yet, even with all his petitions to: improve the militia's quantity and quality; send more regular troops from Britain; build up the navy; and reinforce alliances with the Native tribes; Brock knew his strength would never be in numbers. How could it be when three-fifths of the population of Upper Canada, the weakest part of British North America, was comprised of American expatriates! Yet, like his hero Lord Nelson, he welcomed his soldier's fate, even if it meant his doom. Luckily for Brock, his adversary was not nearly as comfortable with his own mortality.

Brigadier-General William Hull expected to be embraced by the people of Canada when he entered Sandwich Town on the bright and sunny Sunday of July 12, 1812. For a military commander leading such an important mission, it's amazing how fragile his constitution was (though he was in his late 50s, many of his soldiers believed him to be at least 70 and nicknamed him "granny"). He even issued a proclamation, intended to both dissuade militia resistance and draw the inhabitants toward his cause: "...the arrival of an army of Friends must be hailed by you with a cordial welcome, You will be emancipated from Tyranny and oppression and restored to the dignified status of freemen."

Brock worried about this attempt at psychological warfare, by which "the disaffected became more audacious, and the wavering more terrified." However, the farm boys of the Upper Canadian borderland were not revolutionaries, nor were they much oppressed. The province offered cheap, fertile land, didn't disturb its inhabitants and its residents paid no taxes—there's a reason there was no "York Tea Party. " Thus, in most cases, the status quo prevailed. Moreover, these people were not the Americans' greatest threat. That honour belonged to the Indian "savages" and their charismatic leader, Tecumseh, whom Hull feared more than all the hard-drinking and harder-fighting career soldiers of the 49th Regiment put together.

It's not surprising then, that when Porter Hanks, an American lieutenant captaining a ship full of dejected American citizens and paroled soldiers, from Michillimakinac Island, Michigan, informed Hull of the capture of their tiny but strategic trading post, by a horde of Indians led by Scotsman-turned-wild-man Robert Dickson, Hull pulled up stakes and retreated to the safety of Fort Detroit.

Brock was well aware of the bitter enmity between the Americans and Natives, as well as the reputation of Tecumseh, who had managed to unite more than one dozen warring tribes of the Northwest into an Indian Confederacy, willing to set aside personal differences to fight the hated "Long Knives" (the Natives' derogatory term for "Americans"). The famed Shawnee chief and the British general first met around midnight on August 12, 1812, when Brock arrived at Amherstburg with 250 York Volunteers after a non-stop, seven-day journey marching through forests and paddling up Lake Erie in leaky boats. It seems that each man was immediately impressed with the other.

Of Tecumseh, Brock wrote: "a more sagacious and gallant Warrior does not I believe exist. He was the admiration of everyone who conversed with him...." Tecumseh's assessment of Brock was more to the point. "This," he later told his followers, "is a *man*!"

But Brock had little time for idle banter or delay, which his vacillating officers were wont to do. When they urged caution and argued that a river crossing with so few men was too risky, he retorted, "We are committed to a war in which the enemy will *always* surpass us in numbers, equipment and resources." Trusting their leader, the officers conceded, and in a few days, Brock, Tecumseh and their men stormed Fort Detroit.

Meanwhile, in the American camp, the situation was completely opposite. Hull's officers had lost all confidence in him, and the whisper of mutiny spread down the ranks like wildfire. Colonel Lewis Cass, one of the instigators of a round robin, even wrote the governor of Ohio, imploring him to come to Detroit with 2000 troops, hoping against hope that he would replace their general. Few realized how tortured Hull's mind was, preoccupied with dwindling supplies, the disorder of his army and the large number of Detroit villagers who had taken refuge within the fort's walls. Still, those fears paled in comparison to his paranoia over an impending attack by "thousands of painted savages," who he felt were drawing ever closer. To Brock's delight, Hull was duped by a phoney letter, intercepted en route to Robert Dickson at Michillimakinac, informing him that "British forces facing Hull are so strong, you needn't send more than 5000 Indians." (In reality, there were only a few hundred Indians there, "as drunk as 10,000 devils," according to one account, and in no shape to fight anything beyond a hangover.)

Sensing an opportunity, Brock sent two aides across the river bearing a white flag and a message, but not of truce: "The force at my disposal authorizes me to require of you the immediate surrender of Fort Detroit....It is far from my intention to join in *a war of extermination*; but you must be aware that the numerous body of Indians which have attached themselves to my troops will be beyond my control the moment the contest commences...."

Hull refused to back down just yet, but the damage was done. Never mind that the force at Brock's disposal barely exceeded 1000 men, most of them Natives, whose tomahawks, though sharp, would be of little use against the walls of a fort. In the end, the mere threat of being captured by Indians, most of whom *did* intend to join a war of extermination, down to the last woman and child if possible, proved to be too much for Hull.

So when the cannonball-lit night sky of August 15 gave way to the red dawn of August 16, it was with perfect timing that Brock and his men stealthily forded the Detroit River. Within a few hours, a practically catatonic American commander, badly shaken after seeing Porter Hanks, the lieutenant from Michillimakinac, cut in two by a 16-pound cannonball and fearing for the safety of the women and children (including his own daughter), raised the white flag and capitulated— to the horror of his own soldiers and astonishment of Canada's defenders.

The victory devastated U.S. morale and initiated Brock to the pantheon of great Canadians. (For his perceived cowardice, Hull was court-martialled and sentenced to be shot, only to be spared for his contributions during the Revolutionary War.) This "bloodless battle" is what captivated the minds of Upper and Lower Canadians, not to mention the many Native groups who had originally chosen neutrality. For the first time in history, this mutually distrustful group of people was unified against a common enemy. Even the untimely tragedy that befell Brock at the legendary Battle of Queenston Heights failed to dampen their resolve.

For, on October 13, 1812, at the most famous battle on Canadian soil in history, Major-General Sir Isaac Brock died while valiantly, though foolishly, leading a charge to recapture the British guns on a promontory near the top of the famously steep, rocky hill at Queenston, mistakenly left unprotected. Always one to lead by example, he was at the head of the suicidal assault when an enemy soldier hiding behind some bushes caught him in the sights of his long rifle. The general was a considerable target, being tall as a maple tree and just as dazzling, with his bright red tunic, golden epaulettes and shining buttons. Unfortunately, he was just as easily felled, and expired instantly when the American's lethal bullet struck him squarely in the chest.

Rallying behind their fallen commander, the defenders of Canada, under Major-General Sheaffe, eventually won the battle that day, killing or injuring about 300 Americans and capturing almost 1000 out of a total 6500 enemy troops. In contrast, the 2200 Canadian defenders suffered much lighter losses—14 dead and about 100 injured or missing—save for the loss of their leader.

Brock's passing touched the hearts of the peoples on both sides of the conflict. On the way to his final resting place, his solemn funeral procession passed through a double line of 5000 army regulars, militia and Natives. Guns boomed every minute, including those on the American side at Niagara and Lewiston, causing Sheaffe to remark, his voice quavering with emotion: "noble-minded as General Brock was, he would have ordered the same had a like disaster befallen the enemy."

At Queenston Heights today, towering 40 metres over the Niagara River, the memory of Brock's sacrifice is preserved, almost 200 years after his death, by the grand monument that marks his grave. It also pays tribute to his amazing life.

Though the War of 1812 would end in stalemate and be largely forgotten after the horror of the two World Wars, the reverberations of Brock's leadership and his ultimate sacrifice are still felt today. He contributed immensely to Canada's national identity, cemented its relationship with the U.S. as an ally worthy of respect, and in 1867, this legacy helped persuade Britain to accept Canada's right to self-determination.

CHAPTER TWO

Tecumseh
(1768–1813)

Sell a country! Why not sell the air, the clouds and the great sea, as well as the earth? Did not the Great Spirit make them all for his children?

–Tecumseh, Vincennes, Indiana Territory,
August 10, 1810

IN THE LONG, MELANCHOLY HISTORY OF BOTH Native and European peoples in North America, the story of the Shawnee Nation—contact and trade, illness and war, making and breaking of land treaties and finally, displacement to the fringes of society—is hardly unique. However, in the late 18th century, there arose from the Shawnee people a brilliant war chief whose strong leadership and radical philosophy promised, at least temporarily, to stem the tide of European incursion steadily eroding Native society. His ascendancy, from humble beginnings to the head of a great First Nation army, would bring bright hopes to his people, with whom he hoped to create a confederacy spanning from the Gulf of Mexico to the Great Lakes. He is, perhaps, the most famous Native son of all: Tecumseh, "The Shooting Star."

In his time, Tecumseh was renowned as one of the finest orators, politicians and generals of his or any other race. His concepts of First Nation union, communal land ownership and the inviolable nature of Native land rights, put him centuries ahead of his time. He argued that no chief of any one tribe had the right to sell land out from under his peoples' feet to any white men or their governments because the land belonged to and was shared by all Natives collectively.

Even his arch-enemy, Indiana Territory governor and short-lived U.S. president, William Henry Harrison, could not help but give credit where it was due, calling his rival:

> ...one of those uncommon geniuses, which spring up occasionally to produce revolutions and overturn the established order of things. If it were not for the vicinity of the United States, he would perhaps be the founder of an Empire that would rival in glory that of Mexico or Peru.

So who was this so-called "noble savage," and more importantly, why is he celebrated simultaneously as a hero to Canadians, Natives *and* Americans? For the most part, he was an enigma. Although he was born and lived most of his life in what today is the United States, he would have certainly loathed being called an American, implying a connection with the terrible "Long Knives" (for the long sabres they carried) who continually plagued his people. Likewise, notwithstanding his enormous—some would say, decisive—contributions to his British and Canadian allies in their War of 1812 "victory," he would have chafed at an association with either nationality. One could argue that even his Shawnee identity was tenuous—he was half-Creek Indian—and, indeed, some of his worst adversaries were Shawnees from rival clans. He may have been a man of contradictions, but he was resolutely a man of the people, a revolutionary who fought for the freedom, equality and happiness of his Native brethren, whether they wanted it or not. For clarification, it is not necessary to look further than Tecumseh's own words:

> It is true I am a Shawnee. My forefathers were warriors. Their son is a warrior. From them I take only my existence. From my tribe I take nothing. I am the maker of my own fortune. And oh! That I might make that of my red people, and of my country, as great as the conceptions of my mind, when I think of the Spirit that rules the Universe.

Tecumseh was born in 1768 (the exact date is unknown), in Old Piqua, which was then a Shawnee village on the Mad River in western Ohio. He was the fifth of nine children born to a Shawnee father named Puckeshinwa and a Creek mother from Alabama named Methoataske, who had met when some Shawnee tribes fled to Alabama during the French and Indian War. Puckeshinwa, a leading war chief among his people, was killed fighting British Virginians in Ohio in 1774. In 1779, when a nearby village was raided by Kentucky militiamen, Methoataske and her youngest daughter fled Ohio with other, pacific-minded, Shawnees to south-eastern Missouri, leaving her remaining children, including Tecumseh, behind.

Although he was an orphaned, middle child whose formative years coincided with the wide-spread violence of the American Revolutionary War, Tecumseh was a well-adjusted boy. His elder siblings particularly adored him. His elder sister, Tecumpease, became his adopted mother, and Chiksika, his older brother, was his warrior role model. It was Chiksika who handed down to Tecumseh their father's legacy of eternal struggle with the Long Knives. And yet, when Chiksika gave him his first chance to join a real war party at 14, Tecumseh was not nearly as bold. In fact, when he witnessed his older brother receive a superficial gunshot wound in a melee with some Kentuckians, Tecumseh recoiled at the sight of blood and fled his position.

It would be his only recorded act of cowardice because he subsequently went to great lengths to prove the extent of his courage. In 1783, at age 15, he partook in an expedition to raid supply and set-tler transports on the Ohio and Licking rivers, where his bravery apparently outstripped even sea-soned fighters. Yet, unlike his fellow warriors, his capacity for ruthlessness on the battlefield did not translate to a lack of humanity where prisoners of war were concerned. Indiscriminate torture was the norm among both Natives and whites in frontier warfare. Bludgeoning, scalping, mutilating and worse were routine punishments for defeated combatants and bystanders, often the prisoners were mutilated while still alive. All this thoroughly disgusted the righteous Tecumseh. After witnessing the members of his war party burn alive a hapless American captive, he vowed to never again allow prisoner torture in his midst.

However, this compassionate streak did nothing to dampen Tecumseh's resolve for fighting the Long Knives, culprits in the deaths of his father and both his older brothers: Chiksika during a raid gone awry in 1788 and another, Sauwauseekau, in 1794, at the infamous Battle of Fallen Timbers. Here the Americans, led by General "Mad" Anthony Wayne, soundly defeated the British-backed Shawnees, resulting in the humiliating Treaty of Greenville that forced the Shawnees to concede most of their ancestral homeland.

By his 27th birthday, in 1795, Tecumseh was already a respected war chief with a growing number of young, increasingly frustrated, anti-American followers. He was also beginning to show signs of the charisma and physical presence that would captivate the imaginations of both red and white people in later years. There are few reliable descriptions of what Tecumseh looked like, for he refused to ever allow a white man to capture his likeness during his lifetime. However, contemporary evidence suggests that, barring his slightly above average height of 1.7 metres (5'10"), there was nothing remarkable about his appearance, except for having a crooked leg, improperly healed after he fell from a horse in his youth.

Although he had absorbed some aspects of European culture in his youth, including the odd swig of whisky, by the time he was in his 30s, Tecumseh had become largely immune to the temptations of white society. He shunned the whites' clothing and sedentary lifestyle that was gaining popularity among his people, and he was vehemently opposed to the scourge of "firewater" that so tormented his fellow Natives, including his younger, misfit brother, Lalawethika.

Lalawethika was the polar opposite of Tecumseh— a poor fighter and useless hunter, rarely able to provide for his family. He had even lost the use of one eye while sharpening an arrowhead in his teens. This outcast sibling was especially vulnerable to the lure of alcohol's blissful haze. However, in 1805, he became the linchpin in Tecumseh's legend after being miraculously cured of the "white man poison" following a mysterious seizure. From this experience, where he claimed to have met and received instruction from the Master of Life while comatose, he emerged reborn as Tenskwatawa (Shawnee for "The Open Door," a saying used by Jesus and showing possible influence from nearby Quaker missionaries). Better known as The Prophet, Tenskwatawa began a popular religious

movement that coincided with Tecumseh's bud-
ding campaign for political union between the
tribes of the Northwest U.S., the one very much
bolstering the other with ideas and devotees.
After some early scepticism, Tecumseh himself
became a convert.

Among other things, a good deal of the
Prophet's "new" religion revived the adherence to
traditional ways of life, which invariably widened
the friendship gap between Natives and the Long
Knives. With the help of Tecumseh, the Prophet
started a religious community in the spring of 1808
on the shores of the bountiful Tippecanoe Creek in
Indiana, dubbed Prophetstown by the surrounding
settlers. Not surprisingly, his moral preachings
reinforced many of the political convictions
Tecumseh preached to his own followers. Both
understood that an overreliance on white, particularly American, culture (and therefore, goods)
would only increase their subservience to American
traders. Although, as a matter of necessity, main-
taining ties with white British traders in Canada
was vigorously endorsed, since they still needed
guns and ammo to fight the Long Knives.

The British were all too happy to meet with
Tecumseh on June 8, 1808. They encouraged the
Native tribes of the Northwest—Wyandot, Seneca,
Sac, Fox, Ottawa, Potawatomi, Chickasaw, Choctaw,
Creek, Kicapoo, Delaware and Shawnee—to join
Tecumseh's Confederacy, if it meant having a
stronger ally in the war looming over the horizon

(the War of 1812). However, being not quite yet on the eve of battle, the political leaders of Upper and Lower Canada worried that their Indian Department representatives, nearly all of whom had Native brides and some of whom were living among their wives' families, would influence the Natives into fighting a proxy war against the U.S. Inevitably, this is what happened following events that took place in Vincennes, Indiana, on September 30, 1809.

While Tecumseh was conveniently out of state, Indiana Governor Harrison assembled a group of U.S.-friendly (as well as liquored and bribed) chiefs, all hostile to Tecumseh, to sign the Treaty of Fort Wayne (even though one of the signatories' tribes didn't even live in the area). Harrison's scheme transferred over 12,000 square kilometres of Native land to the U.S., in exchange for the promise of regular annuities to the tribes of the document's signatories. In total, the tract was bought for about US $50,000 and sold to settlers for US $3 million, nearly 60 times more than the Natives received (about US $550,000 and US $33 billion respectively, in today's dollars).

By the spring of 1810 hundreds of outraged Natives of every stripe were descending on Prophetstown, and with Tecumseh recruiting warriors in several states, many more would soon arrive. But in July 1811, while Tecumseh was still gathering recruits in the Mississippi Valley, the U.S. government decided to act first. Fearing an

uprising by the increasingly brazen residents of
Prophetstown, President James Madison gave Harrison command of an army regiment, with orders
to protect American interests in the area, avoiding
unnecessary bloodshed—if possible. Harrison
chose a very loose interpretation of these orders
when, in early November of that year, he set up
camp with 1000 volunteer and regular soldiers on
the Tippecanoe River directly across from Prophetstown, hoping to goad his enemies into battle.

Tecumseh had similarly ordered his subjects to
refrain from engaging in any hostilities while he
was away. However, Tenskwatawa, certain that the
Master of Life had made him invulnerable to
American bullets, decided to accept Harrison's
challenge and launched a surprise dawn attack. As
an experienced Indian-fighter, Harrison was well
prepared for the attack. The ensuing contest ended
in a draw, a devastating blow for the supposedly
invincible Prophet, whose much-vaunted "medi-
cine" had failed to prevent casualties in his camp.
With many of his followers deserting him for their
old pro-U.S. chiefs, the Prophet was forced to
gather his remaining followers and flee before the
Long Knives could seek retribution. The abandon-
ment of Prophetstown ruined Tenskwatawa as a
shaman. It was also when Tecumseh's carefully
woven Native alliance began to unravel.

But when the British sought allies to stop the
American invasion of Upper Canada in 1812, Tecumseh was still powerful enough to rally a multi-tribal

force of over 600 warriors around his impassioned
war cry:

> [The Americans] *suddenly came against us*
> *with a great force while I was absent and destroyed*
> *our village and slew our warriors…They came to*
> *us hungry and cut off the hands of our brothers,*
> *who gave them corn. We gave them rivers of fish*
> *and they poisoned our fountains. We gave them*
> *forest-clad mountains and valleys full of game*
> *and, in return, what did they give our warriors*
> *and our women? Rum and trinkets and a grave!*

On July 12, 1812, when the spirits of Upper
Canadians were at their lowest ebb after being
invaded and pillaged by the American army under
Brigadier-General William Hull, Tecumseh scored
one of the allies' first victories at Brownstown,
Michigan. Lying hidden in a field of corn, near the
only crossing point on Brownstown Creek,
Tecumseh's tiny contingent of 20 Shawnee and
Ottawa braves and Alexander Elliot, the son of a
British Indian agent, managed to successfully
ambush about 400 American soldiers, killing 18,
wounding 20 and scattering the rest. The Americans had been sent by the brigadier-general to
escort a badly needed wagon train of supplies wait-
ing at the River Raisin and to deliver the army's
mail, including his intelligence reports, to Secretary
of War Henry Dearborn. The supply train never
made it to Hull's camp, and the captured corre-
spondences proved invaluable to the British command, giving them their first indication of the

discontent among enemy ranks and the Americans' dire straits, as imagined by Hull.

Tecumseh thoroughly impressed the British at Fort Malden in Amherstburg, troops and commanders alike, including that other great hero of the war, Major-General Sir Isaac Brock, who called him the "Wellington of the Indians" and future novelist, John Richardson, then a 15-year-old volunteer, who would write of Tecumseh: "there was that ardour of expression in his eye... that could not fail to endear him to the soldiers' hearts."

Tecumseh's actions affected American hearts as well, though with a decidedly opposite effect—it absolutely terrified them! At face value, the Natives' actions in the capture of Fort Detroit would seem minimal. To give the impression of greater numbers, Tecumseh had his followers yell war cries while running in and out of the woods adjacent to the fort three times. Yet, this had the effect of chilling the souls of many troops, especially Brigadier-General Hull. Although he commanded a force of almost 2200 well-armed men from a fortified position, Hull's waking nightmare—that, upon defeat, Tecumseh's vengeful followers would test the sharpness of their knives on American scalps—caused him to surrender on August 16, 1812, with barely a shot fired. Although Brock, who would die only two months later at the Battle of Queenston Heights, would henceforth be known as the "Saviour of Upper

Canada," Tecumseh was equally deserving of that title and became just as famous in his own right.

These and future victories heartened some previously neutral Native tribes to join Tecumseh and the British in fighting the Long Knives, while others were inspired to wage their own independent guerrilla wars. Unfortunately, Major-General Brock's replacement, Colonel Henry Procter, was an ineffectual commander and had none of the rapport with the Natives that his predecessor enjoyed, compounding the dilemma of the allies' slowly reversing fortunes. On May 5, 1813, Procter and Tecumseh managed to share a quasi-victory over the latter's nemesis, Governor William Henry Harrison, now a general, at the Battle of Fort Meigs. A detachment of 800 U.S. troops sent to reinforce the fort was soundly defeated, but the fort, like its tenacious commander, would not give in to the allies and withstood four days of continuous cannon and mortar fire.

It was Harrison who led the second invasion of Upper Canada in August 1813, buoyed by newfound U.S. supremacy over the Great Lakes following the destruction of the British fleet at Put-in-Bay, Ohio, and his recent appointment as commander of the army of the Northwest. Two months later, on October 5, Harrison and a force of 3300 U.S. army regulars, volunteers and militia led the fateful charge against Tecumseh's and the British forces at Moraviantown, a small religious community on the Thames River in Upper Canada.

The 450-strong British resistance lasted all of five minutes. When the troops surrendered, Procter had already retreated on horseback to his command post, strategically placed some distance from the actual battle scene. For their part, Tecumseh and his estimated 700–800 warriors stood their ground, but like their society as a whole, their bravest efforts only delayed the inevitable. The Natives were defeated, and Tecumseh, destined to be a tragic hero, was killed, his dreams of Confederacy dying with him.

There has never been an accurate account of how Tecumseh died or what happened to his body. Native oral tradition says he was hit by an enemy soldier's bullet, and his body was spirited away by comrades to be buried in a secret location, protecting it from white men's morbid curiosity. (Many Natives whose bodies were left on the battlefield had their corpses mutilated by American soldiers looking for macabre souvenirs to take home, which they all invariably purported to have carved from Tecumseh's own flesh.) The popular American account is that Tecumseh had attacked Colonel Richard M. Johnson with a tomahawk and was killed by the latter with a single shot from the colonel's pistol (a story often repeated by Johnson, a Kentucky congressman, and later senator and vice-president, who used the tale to further his political career).

Whatever the truth may be, the memory of Tecumseh's resplendent life far outshines that of his death. There have been numerous claims that, on the eve of his final combat, Tecumseh had a premonition of his own demise and the hopelessness of his cause, but on his last day on Earth, the Shawnee leader seemed oddly calm, if a bit reflective. Perhaps he was recalling his own words:

> *When it comes your time to die, be not like those whose hearts are filled with the fear of death, so that when their time comes they weep and pray for a little more time to live their lives over again in a different way. Sing your death song and die like a hero going home.*

CHAPTER THREE

Laura Secord, née Ingersoll
(1775–1868)

ASK A CANADIAN WHAT LAURA SECORD means to them,
and you'll likely be served a big scoop of sugary
nostalgia about the chocolate and ice cream treats
that concluded many a childhood shopping experience. If prodded further, some patriotic trivia buffs
might recall an old grade-school homework
assignment or *Canadian Heritage Moment* TV com-
mercial, summing up the flesh-and-blood sweetheart of Canadian lore as: "That quaint little lady
in the drab pioneer dress who trudged through
forest and swamp, possibly with a cow (whose
milk may or may not have been required for the
production of chocolate), and managed to save
Canada by warning our army about an attack."

Not quite. Laura Secord is often referred to as
the Canadian heroine of the War of 1812, but
as is so often the case with historical figures, her
tale has been variously adored, propagandized,
ridiculed and disregarded, often out of proportion
to its importance within the conflict in question.
Historians still debate the veracity of the Laura
Secord myth—there was no bovine accomplice, for

example—but much of it is true. She did overhear an American plot to ambush a small group of British soldiers under Lieutenant James FitzGibbon and walked 32 kilometres under extreme conditions to warn him. But to what effect? Was her amateur espionage really what clinched American defeat at the (fairly minor) Battle of Beaver Dams? Moreover, should she still be considered a heroine if it didn't? Indeed, isn't it a greater injustice that the battle's true victors—the Caughnawaga Natives from present day Kahnawake, Québec—are only vaguely remembered for the decisive role they played?

In truth, beneath all the hoopla and hyperbole, Laura Secord was just a person who tried to do right by her country. Regardless of the level of danger she faced on her walk or the effect her warning had on either the Battle of Beaver Dams or the larger war, the act itself was a truly brave and commendable deed. Especially when one considers that she could have just as easily done nothing, leaving the fates of the British and Natives to divine providence.

Laura Ingersoll was born on September 13, 1775, in Great Barrington, Maryland, near the New York border, halfway between Albany, New York, and Hartford, Connecticut. She was the first child of 26-year-old Thomas Ingersoll and 19-year-old Elizabeth Dewey, married only seven months earlier (a fact that caused many blushing biographers to list December as her birth month). Laura was born in the auspicious year that saw Britain's Thirteen Colonies erupt into the eight-year chaos that was the Revolutionary War. This divisive war cleaved the colonies into two bitterly opposing factions—the minority Loyalists, who fought to maintain British control, and the majority colonial patriots, who fought for American independence. Anti-British sentiment was especially pronounced in Massachusetts, where the Boston Tea Party of 1773 was still emblazoned in the memory of most, including Laura's father. In 1777, Thomas Ingersoll became an officer in the colony's army, and by war's end in 1783, had risen to the rank of captain.

Ending the war on the winning side should have been cause for celebration, but instead, an unexpected tragedy struck the Ingersoll family. Elizabeth Ingersoll passed away suddenly in 1783 at age 27, leaving an eight-year-old Laura to watch over her three younger sisters. After a year of mourning, Laura's father remarried in 1884 and again in 1888, when his second wife died prematurely. His third wife, Sarah Whiting, bore him seven more children, four boys and three girls. If readjusting to this newest family dynamic wasn't enough, in 1795, Laura's father chose to abandon Massachusetts and the republic he had fought for, taking his aggregate family on a long and arduous journey northward to British Upper Canada, where the provincial government was selling large tracts of cheap land in order to boost the population.

To pay for the development of his property (the future site of Ingersoll, Ontario) and to put food on the table, Thomas ran a tavern in Queenston, a busy centre for trading and transportation of goods on the Niagara River that, until about 1797, he and his family called home. Queenston was a small town, and "Ingersoll's Tavern" was a natural meeting place for residents and visitors alike—the tavern even doubled as a Masonic lodge during off hours. This is possibly where Thomas first met Laura's future husband, James Secord, a fellow Freemason and up-and-coming merchant in his early 20s.

James Secord was born in 1773, just two years before his future bride. Like Laura, he was born in what today is called the United States, though unlike her, his father fought for the British during the revolution. As a bachelor, living in a small and tight-knit community like Queenston, James would have undoubtedly taken note of the Ingersolls' eldest daughter. To a casual observer like James, she might have easily been mistaken for a more fragile creature than she was: Laura was a slim, attractive girl of modest height, pale complexioned, with light brown hair and dark, expressive eyes. However, in the crucible of her tumultuous childhood and adolescence, Laura's remarkable hardiness, courage and unwavering resolve were forged—qualities that would serve her so well in the coming years. So, around 1797 (the exact date is unknown), the hard-bitten pioneer and the tender-looking-but-tough lass were wed by James's older brother David, the local Justice of the Peace and founder of St. David's, where James owned a farm and the newlyweds began their life together.

Soon after their nuptials, the Secords moved back to Queenston. James eked out a living there as a wholesaler of farmed goods, but was perpetually in debt, eventually forcing him to mortgage the 80-hectare farm he had inherited from his father.

Little is known of Laura's life during these years of financial instability. She appears on the docket of Niagara's court during James's mortgage dealings when she relinquished her dower— the legal claim she had to *part* of her husband's property if he died. At the time, women were not considered persons under the law and, therefore, technically could not own property (though they could still become national heroes). Laura was certainly busy at the now-famous Laura Secord Homestead that lies at the foot of Queenston Heights, where Laura gave birth to five children: Mary in 1799, Charlotte in 1802, Harriet in 1806, Charles in 1809 and little "Appy," short for Appalonia, in 1810. However, in 1812, the Secords' circle of kith and kin grew smaller by one when Thomas Ingersoll died at the age of 63. Alas, history would allow Laura little time to grieve over the loss of her father, because that same awful year, larger events once again threatened to tear her world asunder.

On June 12, 1812, the War between the United States and Great Britain officially began. But, rather than engage in a naval battle somewhere in the mid-Atlantic, it rapidly became clear that Upper Canada was the theatre where Washington and London intended to perform their gruesome farce. Queenston was particularly vulnerable, the U.S. being just across the Niagara River.

When the hostilities commenced, James Secord, a former militiaman and dyed-in-the-wool Loyalist, didn't hesitate to re-enlist with the First Lincoln Militia regiment, where he held the rank of sergeant. He must have also sensed the danger to his family and possessions and was probably just as motivated by his concerns as a father and husband. His pre-science was well founded because, on October 13, 1812, one of the fiercest battles ever waged on Canadian soil was fought within earshot of the Secord residence—the Battle of Queenston Heights, where Major-General Sir Isaac Brock famously perished. That afternoon, while his panic-stricken wife and children hid in a nearby farmhouse and insolent American soldiers plundered his home and business, Sergeant Secord was seriously wounded. He was a part of a light artillery unit, whose small but deadly guns the Americans definitely wanted silenced. During Major-General Roger Sheaffe's successful recapture of Queenston's steep hill, Sergeant Secord caught some enemy fire. Two bullets hit him, one in the shoulder and another that lodged in his knee, where it remained for the rest of his days.

When the battlefield grew quiet in the late afternoon, Laura decided to venture out of her hideaway to determine the outcome and soon discovered her husband's misfortune. After a mad dash up the hill, Laura was confronted with the agony of locating James from among the many bullet-riddled and bloodied soldiers of both armies, strewn haphazardly over the battlefield like so many dead leaves. When she at last found him, James was bleeding profusely from his shoulder wound. With the help of a sympathetic British officer, the trio hobbled the thankfully short distance to the Secords' ransacked home, where Laura tried to nurse her husband's injuries with the scant resources available to her. However, the increasing momentum of the U.S. war machine quickly overshadowed the Secords' malaise.

Over the course of the winter of 1812 and spring of 1813, the Americans won several key battles in quick succession, gaining possession of the eastern Niagara region, including Queenston. Although the British were able to halt the American advance on the Niagara peninsula on June 6, 1813, at the Battle of Stoney Creek, the Americans were still able to raid the countryside and challenge the British from their stronghold of Fort George (near present-day Niagara-on-the-Lake, Ontario). By the end of June, the Americans were already preparing to ambush the small British detachment under the audacious Lieutenant FitzGibbon, headquartered at the De Cew (pronounced "de cou") house near

Beaver Dams. On June 21, Laura overheard as
much, although no one knows for certain how. The
most popular and plausible account is that she was
able to eavesdrop on the conversation of a group
of American officers billeted at her house (possibly
including Captain Cyrenius Chapin, who particularly disliked the cheeky Irish lieutenant's guerrilla
tactics and is believed to have masterminded the
ambush). It was under these circumstances that
Laura Secord performed her heroic walk.

With the first light of dawn on June 22, 1813,
Laura kissed her children goodbye and set out on
her journey. The night before, she had divulged
the enemy scheme to her husband, who greeted
her news with a mixture of anger and despair.
James Secord was still convalescing from his battle wounds and therefore was in no shape to make
the long walk to De Cew's. So, after some deliberation, they agreed that Laura would have to go it
alone. She was to start off towards St. David's, west
of Queenston, with the pretence of visiting her
half-brother Charles, in case she should be questioned on the way by an American sentry. Charles
had been recovering from a bout of fever at the
home of Hannah Secord, James' sister-in-law and
the mother of Charles' beautiful, but frail fiancée,
Elizabeth. James hoped Charles might be healthy
enough to relay Laura's message to FitzGibbon
himself. Alas, when she arrived that morning at
her sister-in-law's, Charles was still bedridden.
After sitting down to rest her feet, which were

beginning to grow sore from walking in her low-heeled leather house slippers (women's hiking boots had yet to be invented), she, Hannah and Elizabeth decided that it would be too risky to travel on the open road that led directly to Beaver Dams, about 16 kilometres away. Instead, Elizabeth would accompany Laura on the more circuitous route, taking the Swamp Road west to Shipman's Corners (now called St. Catherines) and then following the winding forest path that ran beside Twelve Mile Creek south to De Cew's.

The pair made their way along the mucky and mosquito-infested Swamp Road, and before long, the morning air, cool from the previous night's rain, turned into a hot, muggy summer afternoon. Their smart white bonnets, long homespun dresses and especially their dainty footwear facilitated nothing, save perhaps dehydration and blisters, and made the already difficult trek nearly impossible. Upon reaching Shipman's Corners, Elizabeth knew her weak constitution wouldn't allow her to continue, and rather than hold her aunt back, she bade Laura to continue her mission alone.

Laura had a tough decision to make. She was equally if not more tired than her niece and scarcely knew the way—not to mention her reasonable fear of being waylaid by either hostile Indians, suspicious Americans or any manner of wild animal, from wildcats to rattlesnakes, that inhabited the area. Nevertheless, after receiving some words of encouragement and an embrace from Elizabeth, Laura picked up her skirt and entered the gloomy woods standing between her and her objective. It certainly was no cakewalk. She trudged for several hours in stifling heat over muddy and uneven ground, walking much of the way barefoot after losing or discarding her slippers and having to contend with black flies constantly biting her and branches that caught on her clothing and scratched her face.

As daylight began to fade, so did Laura's hopes, but when she heard the sound of cascading water, she was cheered, knowing she had arrived at De Cew's Falls, and her exhausting 32-kilometre voyage was almost over. After crossing the creek on a fallen tree trunk, Laura was nearing the steep hill where FitzGibbon's headquarters lay when, all of a sudden, she found herself surrounded by a large group of Natives, whose camp she had mistakenly intruded upon. The rest, as they say, is history.

Almost 50 years later, in 1860, an 85-year-old Laura Secord had the opportunity to give an official account of her story, in much more comfortable circumstances, to Queen Victoria's oldest son, Edward, the Prince of Wales and the future King Edward VII:

> *I came to a field belonging to a Mr. [De Cew], in the neighbourhood of the Beaver Dam. By this time, daylight had left me. Here I found all the Indians encamped; by moonlight the scene was terrifying, and to those accustomed to such scenes, might be considered grand. Upon advancing to the*

*Indians, they all rose, and, with some yells, said
"Woman," which made me tremble. I cannot
express the awful feeling it gave me; but I did not
lose my presence of mind. I was determined to per-
severe. I went up to one of the chiefs, made him
understand that I had great news for Captain
FitzGibbon, and that he must let me pass to his
camp, or that he and his party would be all taken.
The chief at first objected to let me pass, but finally
consented, after some hesitation, to go with me and
accompany me to FitzGibbon's station, which was
at the Beaver Dam, where I had an interview with
him. I then told him what I had come for, and
what I had heard—that the Americans intended to
make an attack upon the troops under his command, and would, from their superior numbers,
capture them all.*

FitzGibbon's incredulity of the news was sur-
passed only by his amazement at the messenger!
When he wrote of the unexpected meeting years
later, the lieutenant commended this unlikeliest
of spies, in his own words, "a person of slight and
delicate frame [who] made this effort in weather
excessively warm...exposed to danger from the
enemy, through whose line of communication she
had to pass."

That night, probably as a result of Secord's information, FitzGibbon readied his force of 50 British
regulars and more than 400 Natives for imminent
battle. However, it was not until the following
evening that the Americans left Fort George and

not until the morning of June 24, two days after Secord's warning, that they fought the Battle of Beaver Dams. The battle unfolded on a country road leading to De Cew's cabin, fought almost exclusively by the Caughnawagas under the Lower Canada militia captain, Dominique Ducharme. For three hours, the 180 lightly armed Native fighters, hidden behind bushes and trees, picked off American soldiers as if hunting grouse.

The almost 500-strong U.S. regiment under Lieutenant-Colonel Charles Boerstler was heavily armed, but proved to be ill suited to woodland combat. When the American situation looked bleakest, FitzGibbon decided to offer his adversary a way out—surrender now or face the *far* superior British force and potential massacre at the hands of the even fiercer Six Nation Mohawks. The ruse worked, and for the time being, FitzGibbon and his 50 men became the heroes of the Battle of Beaver Dams, "won without firing a shot." This caused Lieutenant John Norton, chief of the Six Nation Mohawks, to remark famously, and not without irony, "The Cognawagas (*sic*) Indians fought the Battle; the Mohawks or Six Nations got the plunder, and Lieutenant FitzGibbon got the credit."

As for Laura Secord, her share of recognition for the "British" success and for her patriotic devotion following the War of 1812 was equally meagre. FitzGibbon made no mention of her in any of his official dispatches, and the press did not cover her story at the time. Not that she walked away empty-handed. Prince Edward was so thoroughly impressed with Secord's tale that, a few months after their encounter in 1860, he sent her £100 in gold coins (worth about £5800, or $13,000 Canadian at 2002 exchange rates). Fortunately, the coins weren't foil-covered chocolates.

Laura Secord died a few years later in 1868 at the age of 93 and is buried in Drummond Hill Cemetery, where a monument now stands in her honour. The landmark Laura Secord Homestead, owned since 1968 by Laura Secord Inc. (based, ironically, in Boston, Massachusetts) was made a public trust in 1998 and is now operated by the Niagara Parks Commission. In 2003, the Ministry of Canadian Heritage designated her a "Person of National Historic Significance" for her bravery in the War of 1812.

CHAPTER FOUR

Louis-Joseph, Marquis de Montcalm
(1712–1759)

DEPENDING ON WHERE YOUR ALLEGIANCES lay in the mid-18th century, he was either a brilliant general or a war criminal, a man of the people or an aloof Old World aristocrat, divinely blessed or just plain lucky. Today, he is remembered as both a war hero and war loser. It's only fitting that someone with such a complicated background would bear the tongue-twisting moniker Louis-Joseph de Montcalm-Gozon, marquis de Montcalm, seigneur de Saint-Véran, Candiac, Tournemine, Vestric, Saint-Julien et Arpaon, baron de Gabriac et général majeur des armées françaises en Nouvelle-France. Although his tenure as de facto commander of France's North American army lasted only three years, reverberations from his life and actions during that time are still felt today. Without a doubt, there are few events that have left as indelible a mark on Canada's character as Montcalm's tragic defeat on the Plains of Abraham almost two and a half centuries ago.

In the words of historian Francis Parkman, "Measured by the numbers engaged, the Battle of

Québec was but a heavy skirmish; measured by results, it was one of the great battles of the world."

On February 29, 1712, at the Château de Candiac, near Nîmes in southern France, Louis-Joseph de Montcalm was born to Louis-Daniel de Montcalm and Marie-Thérèse de Lauris. Six years later, Louis-Joseph was sent to study under his father's half-brother, Louis Dumas. The young pupil decried his uncle's strict methods to his parents on several occasions, but by the time he was 14, the obstinate student was well versed in Greek, Latin and history, though he would never quite master written French, thwarting his aspirations for a career at the prestigious *Académie française*. Dreams of an academic life aside, Montcalm had a warrior's destiny to fulfil.

There was an old saying among the country folk of the hamlets surrounding Candiac that "war was the tomb of the Montcalms." Indeed, the Montcalm family tree was laden with noble warriors, including Dieudonné de Gozon, the legendary Grandmaster of the Order of St. John who, according to myth, slew the dragon of Rhodes. So in 1727, at age 15, Louis-Joseph took up the mantle of his ancestors, entering the army as an ensign in the regiment of Hainaut, followed by the purchase of a captaincy two years later. In 1733, France became embroiled in the minor Polish War of Succession, and that year, 21-year-old Captain Montcalm received his trial by fire during the

French capture of Kehl, across the Rhine from Strasbourg, Alsace and again the following year at the siege of Philippsbourg in the neighbouring region of Lorraine. The war ended successfully for France, and in 1735, Montcalm went home to Candiac. Rather than celebrate, he returned to mourn the death of his father, who had passed away that year, and to collect his inheritance—including the substantial debt that his father had left behind.

Not coincidentally, Louis-Joseph, now an elaborately titled but economically-troubled marquis, was strategically married a year later, in 1736, to a noblewoman three years his senior. His bride, 27-year-old Angélique-Louise Talon du Boulay, had a modest estate and influential ties—her great-uncle, Jean Talon, had been the first Intendant of New France. Practicality of the union aside, Montcalm seemed to have truly loved his wife. The deep bond he shared with *la marquise de Montcalm*, the mother of his 10 children, is shown by the many letters he wrote to her in later years, speaking always in loving terms of "my heart," "my love" or "my dearest." Regrettably, officers such as Montcalm only sporadically enjoyed family life and repose, and for seven years, beginning in mid-1741, he was off fighting in various campaigns all over Europe in the Austrian War of Succession. He gained valuable experience as a military leader and strategist during these years, not to mention being made a Knight of St. Louis in 1741 and receiving a promotion to colonel of the regiment of Auxerrois in 1743.

But war was not without hazards: he came perilously close to starving to death in Prague at the beginning of the war and twice cheated death on the Italian peninsula. At the doomed assault on Piacenza, he repeatedly rallied his troops, only to receive three bullet wounds and five sabre cuts for his troubles—including a matching pair of gashes to the head—and was then captured and imprisoned. He was promoted to brigadier-general upon his parole to France a year later, in 1747, and quickly returned to the fray, where he was once again wounded, this time by an enemy musket ball. The largely futile war ended on October 18, 1748, with the belligerent parties signing the general peace of Aix-la-Chapelle, and Montcalm resumed life with his family.

His exploits had not gone unnoticed. In February 1756, an ominous letter from Paris arrived at the Château de Candiac, affixed with a royal seal. It was addressed to the Marquis de Montcalm from d'Argenson, the Minister of War:

> At Versailles, January 25th, midnight....The choice of the king has fallen upon you for the command of his troops in North America, and he will honour you on the occasion of your departure with the rank of major-general.

France's tenuous claims to North America's two most precious waterways—the Ohio-Mississippi and St. Lawrence-Great Lakes—were being challenged by Britain's Thirteen Colonies. New France encompassed almost half of North America, but was populated by no more than 60,000 people, protected by a threadbare chain of fortifications along the rivers and lakes that stretched from Louisiana to Louisbourg, on Cape Breton Island. Conversely, more than one million people lived in Britain's American colonies living on a small strip of coastal land east of the Appalachians.

Montcalm knew the risks—his wife certainly thought it a fool's errand—but the promises of glory for himself and his eldest son, the Chevalier de Montcalm, who was to be made the head of a regiment, were too great to resist.

On April 3, 1756, Montcalm set sail for New France on the *Licorne*. Accompanying him were two battalions, a mere 1200 troops, from the regiments of La Sarre and Royal Roussillion. Meanwhile, in its characteristic myopia, France sent almost 100,000 soldiers to fight on the Austrian front, where they would accomplish nothing. While still in port, he wrote a letter to his mother, in which he displayed (however unconsciously) the prescient understanding that there might not be a return voyage:

> *I have business on hand still. My health is good, and the passage will be a time of rest. I embrace you and my dearest [wife], and my daughters. Love to all the family. I shall write up to the last moment.*

Although it was Easter time, the voyage was no pleasure cruise. The *Licorne*'s passengers endured gale-force winds, punishing waves, innumerable icebergs and unspeakable nausea. The ship finally reached New France on May 13, 1756; however, Montcalm had little time for idle sightseeing. Unbeknownst to him, Britain officially declared its intentions to France two days later, on May 15, 1756. So began the Seven Years' War, the first truly global conflict in history that caused many deaths and countless injuries on five different continents.

Luckily for Montcalm, the land and people he was to defend weren't without advantages. New France's 15,000-strong militia rarely displayed the insubordination so rife within the enemy's ranks—even though the Canadians were unpaid for their services. Also, they enjoyed much better relations with the First Nations than their British counterparts, fostering the creation of extensive alliances and leading to superior Canadian know-how in the art of guerrilla warfare. Added to these were New France's 3000 elite *troupes de terre* (army regulars from France) and 2000 *troupes de la marine* (the colony's standing army)—to say nothing of the landscape's natural defences.

It could even be argued that Montcalm's greatest obstacle was not the British at all. Rather, New France had already been sent careening toward oblivion by Paris's historical indifference to the land that Voltaire derisively referred to as *"quelques arpents de neiges"* (a few acres of snow) and the colony's own despotic administration. Chief among the latter group was the pompous, two-faced and envious Canadian-born governor, Pierre François Rigaud, the Marquis de Vaudreuil. Vaudreuil had been used to running New France like it was his own small fiefdom and was often at loggerheads with the new general, who France had foolishly placed under the governor's direct command. Equally detrimental to Montcalm's cause, if only obliquely, was Vaudreuil's confrere, the notoriously crooked Intendant François Bigot, who stole millions of the King's francs to sustain his luxurious lifestyle of *fêtes* and banquets, while the starving masses subsisted on melted snow and horsemeat.

"What a country!" Montcalm later exclaimed, "Here all the knaves grow rich, and the honest men are ruined."

All the same, our valiant hero fought with his life so the miserable administrations on both sides of the Atlantic could still have a colony to govern. Montcalm won four memorable battles against the British before his fateful showdown with Wolfe on the Plains of Abraham. The first, at Oswego, in 1756, was hard-fought, but handily won; the second, at Fort William Henry, in 1757, was a smashing, if somewhat pyrrhic, victory owing to the massacre of almost 100 prisoners of war by Montcalm's Native allies (which has forever tarnished his image in the eyes of some British and American historians); the third, at Ticonderoga, in 1758, was a life-and-death struggle for Montcalm, won by a combination of guts, inventiveness and luck; and a final, fleeting victory at Montmorency Falls in 1759.

The general's first campaign, in 1756, focused on attacking the three British forts at the mouth of the Oswego River, Britain's westernmost position and its only foothold on Lake Ontario. Montcalm hoped a show of force there would demoralize the British and divert them from French-held Lake Champlain, where 10,000 British soldiers were rumoured to be preparing an assault. The most "sturdy" of the three forts, Fort Ontario, was garrisoned with 600 or 700 men, rumoured to be half-starved and pox-ridden, with a handful of light artillery behind wooden walls, which would be worthless against heavy cannon fire. Almost directly across the river was Old Oswego (Fort Pepperell), whose crude stone and clay walls were just as unlikely to resist a well-aimed artillery round. Meanwhile, not far upstream was the partially completed New Oswego (Fort George), formerly a cattle pen that the British unaffectionately called "Fort Rascal."

Montcalm left Montréal for Fort Frontenac (now Kingston, Ontario) on July 21, 1756, with a detachment from Québec and a band of frighteningly painted and garbed Menomonee from west of Lake Michigan and picking up soldiers along the way to his destination. When the assembly of French *bateaux* at last reached the Oswego under cover of darkness at about midnight, August 10, 1756, they numbered no less than 3000 French and several hundred Canadian and Native fighters. The attackers were discovered the next morning, August 11, but by then it was too late. The Canadians and Natives lurking in the forest aimed a steady barrage of shouts and shots at the fort, while the regular soldiers dug trenches and set up batteries for their two dozen cannon all of that day and most of the next.

The British at Fort Ontario put up a spirited fight with their eight small cannon and single mortar on August 12, but by nightfall on August 13, their bombardment ceased. The French artillery had not yet opened fire, but the British commander at Old Oswego, Colonel Mercer, ordered the garrison to spike their guns and cross over to his side of the river. Undaunted, Montcalm set his men to work once again, digging ditches all night and dragging cannon up to the promontory where the abandoned fort stood. By the morning of August 14, the French began their cannonade from the heights, while a detachment of Canadians and Natives who had crossed the river harassed the British from the ground. With the fort's walls crumbling all around them, the British fought valiantly, but their effort finally collapsed when Colonel Mercer was cut in two by a cannonball. They surrendered at last.

With the loss of only a few dozen men and a few nights' sleep, New France was once again the undisputed Master of the Lakes thanks to the dedication of Montcalm and his soldiers. He later described the extent of the prize in a letter to his mother:

> They yielded themselves prisoners of war to the number of 1700...three military chests full of money, 121 pieces of ordnance, a year's supply of provisions for 3000 men and six decked boats carrying from 4 to 20 guns each.

Before returning to Montréal, Montcalm had the fort and any provisions that could not be carried unceremoniously burned and near the ruin, planted a large cross and a staff bearing the French coat of arms, with the Latin inscriptions: *"In hoc signo vincunt"* (With this sign, they conquer) and the tongue-in-cheek *"Manibus date lilia plenis"* (Give lilies in full hands—a quote from Virgil that played on both the French *fleur-de-lys* and the customary floral funeral offering). Considering the way history turned out, maybe Montcalm realized that these cryptic messages were best applied to his enemies, for it was the British who ended up conquering and he, along with New France, whose imminent death would oblige a fitting epitaph.

For New France, 1757 was a bright, golden year. The fortress at Louisbourg remained impregnable against the British navy, and Montcalm's ceaseless efforts to save the colony paid dividends at the Battle of Fort William Henry. But by 1758, the rot festering behind the gilt façade started to show, and New France's fortunes began an irreversible decline. Prior to this, the Anglo-American war effort had been a comedy of errors, characterized by indecisive or inept leadership and bitter infighting. However, after the cannibalism, mutilation and ransoming of POWs by French-allied Natives at Fort William Henry, the Anglo-American war machine became fuelled with vengeance, and their subsequent string of victories simply added grease to the wheels.

During the summer of 1758, Montcalm managed a heroic victory at the siege of Fort Carillion on the Ticonderoga peninsula of Lake Champlain, over 15,000 British and American soldiers, with a force of only 3000 French regulars (and without any support from Governor Vaudreuil). Unfortunately, the walls began to close in when the British at last captured Louisbourg and then Fort Frontenac, sealing off New France's supply routes from both the Atlantic and Great Lakes.

After the loss of Fort Duquesne (modern-day Pittsburgh) and thus, the whole Ohio Valley, the British had flexed enough muscle to win the fear and respect of many Native tribes, who either pledged neutrality or turned against the French entirely. By 1759, the British juggernaut was unstoppable, when forts Carillion and St-Frédric (Crown Point) fell to the Red Coats, negating Montcalm's successful defence of Lake Champlain just a year before. All that remained was the citadel of Québec.

With nowhere left to run, the fight for New France's last but greatest fortress would be both desperate and fierce. France had basically deserted him, so Montcalm needed the unconditional support of

Vaudreuil and every able-bodied Canadian that could carry a rifle.

Instead of a helping hand, Montcalm received a slap in the face. On September 12, when he ordered 400 soldiers of La Guyenne regiment to guard the cliffs at l'Anse au Foulon against a sneak attack, Vaudreuil, incensed that any order should go over his head, called the troops back and scolded Montcalm with the immortal line: "The English haven't wings! Let La Guyenne stay where it is. I'll see about Foulon myself tomorrow morning."

Early the next fateful morning, September 13, 1759, while Vaudreuil still slept, General Wolfe and his soldiers "grew wings" and made their famous climb up the cliffs.

In just a few hours time, the prized generals of both armies were facing each other at opposite ends of the Plains of Abraham. Montcalm had ordered most of the locally available troops and all 25 of the citadel's field guns to the plain. Vaudreuil again countermanded the order, relinquishing only 3500 men and three artillery pieces. When Montcalm arrived at the battlefield with his eight battalions—about 3500 malnourished, exhausted and poorly equipped soldiers—Wolfe already had 3300 soldiers of his well-provisioned army and some artillery in position, with reserves of at least 2000 men and the British navy close by.

Had Montcalm waited for reinforcements, which were less than an hour away, he could have doubled the size of his force and the course of North American history might have turned out differently. But he had little cause to believe help would ever arrive. Instead, the defiant general— fittingly costumed for his final act in full military regalia astride his favourite black steed—decided to make a final, desperate charge against his Britannic foes. It was an utter failure.

The French were decimated by an endless wave of well-orchestrated British rifle and cannon fire, and despite their initial courage, they lost their nerve within a few minutes and began to flee. Montcalm tried to stop the retreat, and he was twice caught in the line of fire. The second shot proved fatal.

Two of his men rushed to his side and held him aloft on his horse all the way back to Québec. When he reached the city, a woman who saw the blood flowing down his coat shrieked, "Oh my God! My God! The marquis is killed!" to which Montcalm, not realizing the mortal wound to New France that the bullet had wrought, responded, "It is nothing, nothing at all. Do not trouble yourselves over me, my good friends."

The war raged on for another four years, but the fate of New France and the French-speaking inhabitants of North America was largely sealed when their guardian succumbed to his battle wounds on the morning of September 14, 1759.

"It was a sad spectacle..." wrote Captain de Foligné, after witnessing the battle from the *Hôpital-général de Québec*, "I would have never thought that the loss of a general could have caused a rout which, I venture to say is unparalleled."

Fittingly, on October 22, 2001, Montcalm's remains were moved from Québec's Ursuline convent, to the old *Hôpital-général*'s cemetery, where he now rests among the graves of his soldiers.

CHAPTER FIVE

Alexander Roberts Dunn
(1833 –1868)

Forward, the Light Brigade!
Was there a man dismayed?
Not though the soldier knew
Some one had blundered:
Theirs not to make reply,
Theirs not to reason why,
Theirs but to do and die:
Into the Valley of Death
Rode the six hundred
–Alfred, Lord Tennyson's *Charge of the Light Brigade*

"FOR VALOUR"—PERHAPS THE MOST SUCCINCT argument why soldiers like Alexander Roberts Dunn so deserve our highest esteem. It is for their raw, sincere valour, their superhuman perseverance and self-sacrifice that we distinguish these rare heroes from the rest of humankind. Queen Victoria understood this when she had the motto inscribed onto the Victoria Cross (VC), the British Commonwealth's first medal to exclusively reward military valour. Created in 1856, the VC is now considered to be the pre-eminent military decoration for conspicuous courage "in the face of the enemy." Only 1354

have ever been awarded, 96 to Canadians. Dunn
was one of the original recipients and is the first
Canadian winner of the VC for his daring rescue of
two fallen comrades in the waning moments of the
Charge of the Light Brigade during the Crimean War.
In fact, the idea for the honour arose from the ashes
of that colossal gaffe—the military equivalent of
"broken telephone"—where Dunn and 672 fellow
cavalrymen were mistakenly ordered to charge a
gauntlet of Russian artillery. The medals are even
cast in bronze from two Russian cannon captured
during the war. Miraculously, Dunn managed to
walk away from the "Valley of Death" unscathed.
(He also walked away with his commanding officer's
wife!) And he went on to achieve several other
"firsts" for a Canadian soldier—raising a regular
army regiment with all-Canadian recruits, commanding his own regiment and becoming the
youngest colonel in his time. Sadly, fate cut his life
short at age 35 in a dubious hunting accident in
Africa, where it is alleged that he accidentally shot
himself. Sadder still is that, rather than becoming the
Canadian icon he deserves to be, he has instead been
relegated to the dustbin of history (his recently re-
discovered gravesite in Senafe, Eritrea, had become a
makeshift goat pen and refuse dump). So just how
did a unique Canadian icon like Dunn become a
"forgotten hero"? As with so many other things
about this enigmatic figure from Canada's past, it is
quite an intriguing mystery.

Alexander Roberts Dunn was born in York (Toronto) on September 15, 1833, the son of Charlotte Roberts and British-born John Henry Dunn, the receiver general of Upper Canada from 1820 to 1841, and until 1844, York's representative in the provincial legislature. The well-to-do Dunn family lived in an old-fashioned two-storey mansion on a large estate, in a posh neighbourhood near present-day Richmond Street, just west of Spadina. Little is known of Dunn's formative years, except that he was a spirited and athletic youth, if a poor student, at Upper Canada College, and that following his mother's death, he and his father moved back to England, where he continued his education at the elite Harrow School in London.

On March 12, 1852, when Alexander was 19, his father bought him a commission as a cornet (standard bearer) in the 11th Hussars (Prince Albert's Own) light cavalry regiment, one of the most distinguished regiments in the British army at the time. Shortly after he entered the 11th, the regiment was posted to Ireland, where Dunn was promoted to lieutenant the following year, in 1853. By all accounts, Dunn was the ideal cavalryman: he was a natural equestrian, skilled marksman and extremely lethal with a sword. He cut quite an impressive figure physically as well: blond haired, fair complexioned and handsome, sporting one of the large, walrus-like moustaches so fashionable in that bygone era. Although it is said he cultivated a tough, disciplinarian image, he was admired and respected by his men. However, his most striking feature was his exceptional height—at 1.9 metres (6'3") tall, he towered over ally and adversary alike. To take advantage of his long reach, Wilkinson's Swords made him a custom 1.2-metre (4-foot) sabre, many centimetres longer than regulation length. The extra distance this put between Dunn and his adversaries provided him with a bit of insurance, though not enough to be of any comfort where he was going. In May 1854, two months after Britain and France had formed an alliance with the Ottoman Empire and declared war on Russia, the 11th Hussars set sail from the Emerald Isle for Balaklava, on the shores of the Black Sea, where Lieutenant Dunn received his baptism by cannon fire and from thence emerged a hero.

The dawn of October 25, 1854, cast a grey, frosty pall over the Balaklava Plain, the now-infamous battleground, bordered on the south by the allied base of operations at Balaklava's seaport, to the north by the Fedioukine Hills, to the west by Sapoune Ridge and to the east by the Tchernaya River. The plain itself was divided into a North and South Valley by a strategic, but poorly protected, low ridge of hills, dubbed the "Causeway Heights" because of the vital supply route to Sevastopol, the Woronzov Road, that ran along its crest. Inclement weather that morning was complemented by a dismal discovery. A large Russian force, under General Pavel Liprandi, of about

25,000 infantry and cavalry with 78 artillery pieces, was seen advancing on the plain's eastern fringes! As luck (or poor judgment) would have it, the main British force was engaged at Sevastopol, leaving only a few hundred men and about 1500 cavalry to defend the allied base.

At about 10:30 AM, several thousand Russian cavalry crossed over the Causeway Heights into the South Valley, where, astonishingly, they were repulsed by a long, double row of rifle-wielding Scots of the 93rd Highland Regiment standing shoulder-to-shoulder. W.H. Russell, *London Times* reporter, likened this hastily assembled formation to a "thin red streak tipped with a line of steel," later popularized as "the thin red line," which is now synonymous with British, especially Scottish, military gutsiness. As the Russians tried to regroup on the crest of the Causeway Heights, the 800-strong Heavy Cavalry Brigade somehow managed an offensive charge *up* the ridge and succeeded in pushing the Russians back into the North Valley. Bracing for a reprisal, the Russians captured the entrenched artillery positions (redoubts) held by the Turks on the Causeway Heights and set up their own redoubts on the opposite side of the valley atop the Fedioukine Hills. The Russians further defended their position at the eastern end of the valley with a dozen-gun battery, effectively sealing the valley off with a U-shaped wall of heavy cannon and severing the allied lifeline to Sevastopol. With his horde of infantry and cavalry protected by such a formidable barrier, General Liprandi was entirely confident that only a fool or a madman would dare to challenge him. He was right on both counts.

Since the Russian attack had begun, the British field marshal, Lord Raglan, a rusty 65-year-old veteran who hadn't seen combat since Waterloo 40 years earlier, had been watching the ensuing battles unfold from a French lookout on Sapoune Ridge, 200 metres above the plain. The 93rd and Heavy Brigade had slowed the Russians' momentum, but he could see that the enemy was consolidating its forces in the North Valley and had begun hauling away some of the guns protecting the Causeway Heights. Raglan, worried that the Woronzov Road would be lost, issued his famously vague order to the commander of the Cavalry Division: "the cavalry [will] advance rapidly to the front, follow the enemy and try to prevent the enemy from carrying away the gun."

The message passed to Raglan's aide-de-camp, the young hotshot cavalryman, Captain Lewis Nolan, who was further instructed to "Tell Lord Lucan the cavalry is to attack immediately." Nolan rode down the steep hillside with deadly swiftness towards Lucan's camp at the west end of the North Valley. Lieutenant-Genera; Lucan read the puzzling note several times, trying to discern its meaning. From his vantage point on the low ground, the only guns he could see were 12 Russian cannons pointed straight at his camp, protected by several squadrons of cavalry, on the other end of the valley. He had no idea Raglan meant the guns on top of the Causeway Heights, which were outside his field of vision—a deadly oversight on Raglan's part.

Captain Nolan, mindful of the urgency of Lord Raglan's orders, was growing impatient. When Lucan asked him, "What guns?" Nolan flung out his arm in the general direction of the Russians shouting, "There, my Lord! *There* is your enemy! *There* are your guns!" Lucan assumed Raglan wanted a suicidal charge on the guns at the end of the valley, and that's exactly what he ordered Light Brigade commander Lord Cardigan to do, while he followed—at a safe distance with the Heavy Brigade. Cardigan grumbled a bit, acknowledged his orders, assembled his nine squadrons of anxious horsemen and, at 11:20 AM, gave the fateful command: "The Brigade will advance." When the trumpet call for "walk" rang out across the valley, Dunn felt his heart pounding like a drum in his ears and the hair standing up on his neck. Into the Valley of Death he rode, with the 600. Few would ride out.

As the brigade drew closer, to its objective, the Russians poured on the heat, mowing down rows of men and horses with incessant cannon and mortar fire. The front line thinned out, and the ground became littered with mangled corpses, some from being trampled by the charging cavalry as the survivors raced inexorably towards their destination. Allied soldiers in the surrounding vicinity, knowing full well that something had gone terribly awry, watched the action incredulously, gnashing their teeth. French General Pierre Bosquet best summed up the sentiment: *"C'est magnifique, mais ce n'est pas la guerre! C'est la folie!"* ("It's magnificent, but it isn't war! It's madness!")

After facing 10 minutes of point-blank bombardment, the Light Brigade finally made it past the vile row of Russian guns. Lieutenant-Colonel John Douglas led the 80 men that remained of the 11th Hussars, giving his men free reign to release their pent-up rage. Vengeance came crashing onto the fleeing Russian artillerymen like a mighty thunderbolt of British steel, leaving few survivors.

Although the frantic *mêlée* pushed the Russians as far back as the Tchernaya River, the British cavalrymen could only fight for so long with exhausted horses and no infantry support. The 11th Hussars began to retreat, but were challenged by a contingent of Russian lancers. Dunn and the surviving members of his regiment closed ranks and made one final charge to break free of the Russian spears. The Russian line broke at the last moment to let the first, strongest horses through, only to close in and attack the stragglers from the sides. Dunn was one of the cavalrymen who avoided being skewered and could have galloped away to safety, never looking back. Instead, he wheeled his horse around to save the life of Sergeant Robert Bentley, who was being attacked by three Russian dragoons. Sergeant-Major Lloyd Smith witnessed the event, later committing the memory to paper:

> *Dunn fended off the enemy blades, drawing the full fury of their attention against him, allowing time for Bentley to get to his feet. Employing his huge sword, Lieutenant Dunn parried and slashed with effortless strength, and sabred the first dragoon out of his saddle. Although Dunn's horse became almost unmanageable, he and the remaining Russians hacked and circled around until he killed them both.*

Upon dispatching Bentley's attackers, Dunn immediately went to the rescue of another one of his men, Private Levett, killing yet another Russian. (Alas, Levett was himself killed a few minutes later.) The Light Brigade's retreat was mercifully aided (though only belatedly) by the Heavy Brigade, which Lucan had wisely held back after seeing Cardigan's men wantonly sacrificed, and the French *Chasseurs d'Afrique* under General Armand-Octave d'Allonville, who silenced the Russian guns and rifles on the Fedioukine Hills. Nevertheless, Dunn's journey back to camp was still perilous, all the more so because he had to walk back the whole way after his horse gave out from under him.

The aftermath of the half-hour spectacle that was the Charge of the Light Brigade was truly heart wrenching: 156 men were killed or missing, 134 wounded and 14 taken prisoner. The equine death toll was worse still, with almost 500 out of

673 horses killed or subsequently destroyed. Dunn, who somehow hadn't received a scratch, was one of only 25 survivors of the 11th Hussars from an original force of 110. The effects of the "Charge" were felt almost immediately on October 25, 1854. The Light Brigade ceased to exist in the Crimea, Lucan was ruined as a soldier, and Dunn was unanimously voted for a gallantry award. Dunn continued to fight the Russians, participating in the protracted Siege of Sevastopol and the Battle of Inkerman, but his heart wasn't in it anymore—it now belonged to Mrs. Rosa Maria Douglas, the wife of his commander, Lieutenant-Colonel Douglas!

Love trysts in the close living quarters of the battlefield don't stay secret for long, so it must have come as little surprise to Douglas when, shortly after the Charge of the Light Brigade, his not-so-faithful wife of 12 years asked him for a divorce to marry her Canadian lothario. Douglas steadfastly refused, and predictably, Dunn quickly fell out of his commander's favour and was denied the promotion he felt he deserved. He resigned his commission and abandoned the war in 1855. The couple eloped to Canada, where it is presumed they lived together for some time on the Dunn family estate in Toronto, forgetting all about many horrors of the Crimean War. But the world hadn't forgotten about Dunn's heroism.

On June 26, 1857, 24-year-old Lieutenant Dunn was one of 62 soldiers being fêted in a parade at

Hyde Park in London for the first grand Victoria Cross investiture. Queen Victoria herself presided over the illustrious ceremony, and it was she— monarch of the greatest empire ever known, over which the sun never set—who pinned the medal on the breast of Dunn's royal blue hussar jacket. Even though all the fanfare was meant to convey Britain's pride in the heroic exploits of her valiant Crimean War veterans, on another level, it was a masterstroke of public relations artifice—"remember the fighters, forget the fight"—a ploy to clean the slate of the Crimean War and a recruitment tool for Britain's latest conflict, the Indian Mutiny. Indeed, before returning to Canada, Dunn was successfully persuaded to rejoin the army as a major, and he was given the authority to recruit infantrymen in Canada for the first time, into the newly formed 100th Regiment—The Prince of Wales Royal Canadians.

When "Canada's first VC winner" returned to York, he was an instant celebrity. Everyone wanted to meet the dashing, young homegrown war hero, and in no time, he had the 400 recruits he needed to raise his regiment. After a year of intense training, the regiment was posted to Aldershot, England, in the fall of 1858 under Colonel Baron de Rottenburg. It was there that Dunn was presented with the so-called "Sword of General Wolfe," found on the Plains of Abraham. (It is doubted to be authentic, but is nevertheless displayed alongside Dunn's Victoria Cross at Upper

Canada College in Toronto.) After the ceremony ended, de Rottenburg resigned his commission and, at age 27, Dunn assumed command over the 100th as a lieutenant-colonel. The Indian Mutiny had ended by then, and Dunn's regiment was sent to Gibraltar for garrison duty.

Three years later, in 1864, Dunn became a full colonel, making him the first Canadian to command a regiment and the youngest colonel in the British army. However, when his only brother John, a subaltern in the regiment, died of fever that year (leaving him the sole heir to the family fortune), he decided he needed a change of scenery. Dunn transferred into the hard-bitten, globetrotting 33rd Regiment (The Duke of Wellington's Own), which moved from Malta to India and then to Abyssinia (Ethiopia/Eritrea) where it joined General Napier's Expeditionary Force against Emperor Theodore. According to one *London Times* reporter's assessment of the trajectory of Dunn's career at the time, "the highest military appointments [were] within [his] reach."

Yet, before leaving for Africa, Dunn had his own premonition: "I am going to be killed," he told a close friend, "I shall never see England again." On January 25, 1868, in circumstances not all together clear, his fatalistic intuition proved correct. He died that day, at age 33, near Senafe from a gunshot blast.

Speculation abounds as to how he died. Some say his old mistress, Rosa Maria, hired his valet to assassinate him after he had written her out of his will. Others say it was her (or some other mistress') husband exacting revenge. But many believed and still do that lingering depression from the guilt of surviving the Charge of the Light Brigade, coupled with the hard-drinking ways of the 33rd, drove him to suicide. Of course, it is possible that the military coroner's official account is the true one: during a hunting expedition Dunn was sitting on a rock, trying to uncork a brandy flask, when his rifle slipped and the trigger caught on some clothing, firing both barrels into his chest. But because his remains were left in such a remote part of the world, when it was customary to repatriate fallen officers, especially those of Dunn's notoriety, leads to the assumption that the truth lies buried with him, somewhere in East Africa.

In a recent twist to the Dunn mystery, a group of freemasons from Toronto's Ionic Lodge 25, where he was once a member, have been trying to repatriate his remains for several years. (Apparently, the Canadian Department of National Defence wasn't interested.) His remains were recently exhumed and a reinterment ceremony at St. James Cathedral in Toronto was set for October 25, 2004, the 150th anniversary of the Charge of the Light Brigade. As of this writing two months later, what's left of Lieutenant-Colonel Dunn is being held up by customs in Africa. So the saga continues....

CHAPTER SIX

William Avery "Billy" Bishop
(1894–1956)

On the edge of destiny, you must test your strength.

–William Avery "Billy" Bishop

BILLY BISHOP WAS ONE OF ONLY 23,000 Canadian men who served in Britain's Royal Flying Corps (RFC) in World War I—1600 were killed in action and many more injured. He was by no means perfect and would be the first to say so if he were still with us today. As a commander and team player, he was poor to middling at best. As a pilot, his numerous crash landings were the running gag of the air force. He was boastful, prone to exaggeration, and most egregious of all in the eyes of his detractors, he aggressively sought to rack up as many aerial victories as possible, exiting the air force with a whopping 72 victory claims (22 of them with the enemy pilot confirmed by name)—the third highest of any ace and more than any other member of the RFC. Understandably, the popular, high-profile and seemingly unbeatable Canuck rankled some of his more modest (scoring) contemporaries. Sour grapes aside, as Royal Military College historian Lieutenant-Colonel David Bashow put it:

"[Bishop] joined the war effort to kill Germans, not to bake cookies for them."

To fully grasp Bishop's heroism, it is necessary to first know the extreme danger faced by RFC fighter pilots in that still-primitive stage of aviation. British World War I airplanes were essentially wood and canvas contraptions held together with a few screws, not to mention they were also slower and had less firepower than their enemies' aircraft. As well, parachutes came into common usage only late in the war. Even so, Bishop courageously flew over 200 sorties, most of them unaccompanied and deep behind enemy lines, where he often faced down gangs of four or five German fighters and some of their most feared aces, including two clashes with Manfred von Richthofen, the Red Baron. To say he risked his life for his country is an understatement. Truth be told, he was lucky just to have survived the first 11 days of his tour of duty, the average lifespan of a rookie pilot in his squadron! He conveyed the surreal nature of aerial combat in one of the hundreds of letters to his sweetheart, and eventual wife, Margaret Burden:

> *In the air you feel only intense excitement. You cheer and laugh and keep your spirits up. You are all right just after you have landed, as you search your machines for bullet and shrapnel holes. But two hours later, when you are quietly sitting in your billet, you feel a sudden loneliness. You want to lie down and cry.*

Far from being the narcissistic charlatan depicted by his foes, he was a man of complex emotions who cared deeply for his country and his countrymen and continued to do so for the rest of his life, to the tremendous benefit of all Canadians.

William Avery "Billy" Bishop was born on February 8, 1894, in Owen Sound, Ontario, to Margaret Louise Greene and William Bishop, the third son of four children. His father was the registrar for Grey County, an industrious and well-respected gentleman, if a bit strict. Billy's mother was a loving but overbearing type, making the scrawny, blond and blue-eyed boy with a slight lisp go to school in a suit and tie. He preferred swimming, horseback riding and taking dancing lessons to more macho pursuits, which never failed to endear him to the many girls whose company he enjoyed. Needless to say, all the boys at Owen Sound Collegiate mercilessly tormented him. As a result, he was turned off school and became a fearsome schoolyard pugilist. By the time he was a teenager, Billy had shed the "sissy" reputation and was something of a pool shark in the town billiards halls. He also became a crack shot with the 22-calibre hunting rifle his father had bought him for Christmas. (He was such an accomplished squirrel-shooter that the local newspaper dubbed him "the Pied Piper of Owen Sound.") Likewise, his natural prowess with the opposite sex became envied, rather than ridiculed.

When his little sister Louie urged him to take one of her friends from Toronto out dancing—a dainty, auburn-haired girl with hazel eyes named Margaret Burden, whose grandfather was none other than millionaire department store magnate Timothy Eaton—the smug rascal charged her five dollars for the privilege. From that unsentimental beginning, Billy met his future bride.

In February 1911, at age 17, Billy was sent to the Royal Military College in Kingston, Ontario, where his older brother, Worth, had recently graduated with the highest grades of any cadet up until then. Billy's poor high school grades had dashed any hopes of his getting into the University of Toronto and, in any case, everyone felt that a good dose of strict discipline was exactly what the young reprobate needed. With the help of several tutors, he squeaked by the entrance exam and started on his lifelong collision course with military authority. His less-than-stellar performance and constant hijinks did not endear Cadet Bishop to his instructors during his three years at RMC, nor did being caught cheating on his final exam. (He accidentally handed in his crib sheet with his exam!) The threat of expulsion hung over his head during the summer of 1914, but ultimately, his fate was never resolved. On August 4, 1914, Great Britain declared war on Germany, and she needed all the raw recruits her colonies could muster—even a misfit like Billy Bishop.

Bishop's equestrian experience and his education at RMC, however deficient, got him a commission as an officer cadet in the Mississauga Horse militia regiment of Toronto, though a bout of pneumonia kept him from going overseas with his unit. After recovering, he transferred to the 7th Canadian Mounted Rifles, in London, Ontario. But before leaving for England, Bishop screwed up his courage and proposed marriage to Margaret, who duly accepted (though, having forgotten to buy an engagement band, she had to settle for his class ring). On June 9, 1915, Bishop's regiment and their 700 horses left Montréal aboard the *Caledonia* for the rough, perilous—and no doubt smelly—two-week journey to Plymouth, England.

Upon arrival in England, the 7th was sent to Shorncliffe military camp, near the English Channel. The weather was terrible, and the camp grounds were, in Bishop's words, "an incredible morass of muck, mud and mire with the special added unpleasantness that only horses in large quantity can contribute." Bishop realized the folly of using cavalry in trench warfare and quickly became depressed with his prospects. Yet, one fateful summer afternoon in July 1915, an otherwise mundane event profoundly changed his life. A pilot briefly landed his plane in a nearby field and then, having found his bearings, took off again into the sky.

"How long I stood there gazing into the distance I do not know," Bishop later recalled, "but when I turned to slog my way back through the mud, my mind was made up. I knew there was only one place to be on such a day—up above the clouds and in the summer sunshine."

When he was once again sidelined with pneumonia in London, he decided to apply to the RFC, hoping to transfer in as a fighter pilot, though the closest he could get was as an in-flight observer. On September 1, 1915, he went to Netheravon, near Salisbury, for several months of aerial reconnaissance training and on January 1, 1916, was deployed with 21 Squadron at Boisdinghem airfield near St. Omer, France.

By November 1916, after a well-connected friend pulled some strings, he was learning to fly his first plane. Of course, learning to get his plane safely back on the ground was a different matter altogether, as the many British mechanics who dealt with the aftermath of a "Bishop landing" were to discover.

For the duration of the winter of 1916–17, Bishop was relegated to defence patrols in England, until the employment of incendiary bullets put an end to the scourge of Zeppelin bombing raids. At last, on March 17, 1917, he got his wish and then some. He was transferred to 60 Squadron, the top British fighter unit, at Filescamp Farm near Arras, France, the bloodiest theatre for air combat and the hunting ground of the Red Baron's infamous "Flying Circus." Bishop, by then a 23-year-old lieutenant, began flying the Nieuport 17—an improvement over his previous planes, but still mostly inferior to the enemy's Fokker warplanes.

Predictably, he crash-landed on his first sortie on March 25 and barely escaped being sent back to flight school. He fared only a little better on his second outing, when some aerial acrobatics during a dogfight flooded his engine, forcing him to land (amazingly, without wrecking his plane) among the bombed-out craters of No Man's Land. However, he did manage to shoot down his adversary's plane, making it his first victory. Rather than receive a "travel pass" back to training camp, he started leading flight patrols—even though he had only a few hours of experience in the air. He racked up two more victories on his initial forays as flight commander, winning him accolades from the military brass. Sadly, his inexperience as a team leader was also instrumental in the deaths of two rookie pilots and the capture of another. Although his superiors took casualties for granted, the responsibility Bishop felt over these and every other loss under his command weighed heavily on his heart. He put his mind to devising better tactics to ensure that both he and his plane maintained tip-top shape and honed his marksmanship on the firing range.

Bishop's mode of attack became increasingly brazen but also more precise. Staying at a high altitude, preferably behind some cloud cover, the famous eagle-eyed ace took advantage of his uncanny ability to spot prey before he was detected and used the element of surprise to catch German pilots off guard. Once engaged in a dogfight, he preferred efficiency to showy acrobatics—dive in close, fire one or two dozen well-aimed rounds, manoeuvre out of harm's way, then circle around and swoop back to finish the job. Also, like other top fighter pilots, he naturally understood the physics of aerial warfare, like firing *ahead* of an enemy's plane when at a distance, so the aircraft would fly into the bullets' path.

His improved combat techniques proved invaluable during the fourth month of 1917, better known as Bloody April—the second-deadliest month for RFC airmen throughout the entire war. Billy's 60 Squadron was particularly hardhit—the unit had an unthinkable 110 percent casualty rate. (Thirteen of the squadron's original 18 pilots and seven replacements had been shot down.) However, it also added 35 victories to its win column during that brutal period, 12 of which were credited to its leading pilot, Billy Bishop, who was building his own legend as a fighter ace.

Just two weeks after his first disastrous run, on April 7, 1917, he shot down an observation blimp and a fighter plane while flying at a low altitude and sustaining heavy fire from the ground. For this and other acts of "conspicuous gallantry and devotion to duty," to quote the *London Gazette*, he

was awarded a Military Cross. Other gallantry
and service awards eventually followed, as well as
several medals from other allied nations. By the
end of April, with a few more victories under his
belt, he was promoted to captain and was granted
a "roving commission," namely, permission to fly
solo missions into enemy territory (which happened to be his favourite method of "hunting
Huns") alone and unencumbered. It was this
special privilege, afforded only to Britain's top
fighters that gave Bishop the latitude to pull off
the most audacious feat of his career—the legendary pre-dawn aerodrome raid that won him
the Victoria Cross.

Bishop left Filescamp in the early morning of
June 2, 1917, bound for the German aerodrome
at Cambrai. When he arrived there, just before
dawn, he was disappointed to discover that there
wasn't a target in sight. It was raining and visibil-
ity was poor, but he decided to plod on to another
site. After all, he hadn't woken up at 3 AM and
skipped breakfast to go home empty handed! He
flew around and got lost in the thick mist, but
eventually emerged over an airbase, which could
have been Esnes, Estourmel or Awoignt. On the
ground were seven aircraft with engines running.
One pilot had already boarded his plane and was
preparing to take off.

The Germans were caught totally unawares
when Bishop's Nieuport 17 dove at them like a
silver lightning bolt, raking them with fire from

his Lewis machine gun and killing one mechanic. The bold Canuck turned back to strafe the planes again, dodging ground fire from the troops scrambling below, and with another burst of machine-gun fire, he stopped the pilot who was already seated in his aircraft from taking off. He went after another enemy trying desperately to get off the ground, but his aim was off-target. Luckily, a spurt from Bishop's machine gun sufficiently rattled his foe, who accidentally flew into a nearby tree.

So far so good, but Victoria Crosses aren't won so easily. Having wised up to their pursuer's tactics, two more planes took off in opposite directions. Bishop and one of the Germans circled around like a pair of sharks trying to take a bite out of each other's tail. The Nieuport's agility allowed Bishop to sneak under his adversary and empty the rest of his ammunition drum, taking out his adversary's engine and sending him spiralling to earth. The fourth enemy plane was now tearing after him with a vengeance—right when he needed to reload his gun. Unlike the German "Spandau" machine gun, continuously fed by a 550-round ammunition belt, Bishop's 97-round Lewis gun had to be manually reloaded—*in mid-flight*!

Bishop was able to evade his would-be killer and reload his second batch of ammo, which he proceeded to unload on his assailant in one long burst. The bullets missed completely, and the prolonged use overheated his gun. Fortunately, the nervous German pilot gave up the contest and returned to his own airbase. With his gun rendered useless, Bishop jettisoned it to lighten the load on his shredded plane and made a hasty getaway to friendlier territory. On his way back to Filescamp, he ran into a flight of four enemy planes, but miraculously managed to remain hidden until he crossed allied lines and made it safely back to base, just under an hour and a half after he had left it.

Bishop was the only person who could attest to what had happened that morning, as with most of his victories. As a result, some have doubted that the aerodrome raid happened the way he said it did. Some revisionist historians (and one NFB filmmaker) go as far as saying that the whole event never happened and even claim that Bishop shot up his own plane!

Although Bishop's VC is the only one ever awarded without the corroboration of any witnesses, a great deal of circumstantial evidence points to the veracity of his story (and, moreover, a lack of any hard evidence proving the contrary). It took several months of deliberation, but Bishop's story was ultimately accepted by his superiors, not the least of which was because of his reputation as the kind of crazy son of a gun to pull off such a death-defying mission.

Following his VC investiture in August 1917, Bishop was allowed to return to Canada, though not to rest. He was celebrated as a conquering hero wherever he went and became a major war booster at a time when Canadians were sick of losing their sons to an overseas war. He finally married Margaret on October 17, 1917, fittingly, at the Timothy Eaton Memorial Church in Toronto. As soon as the honeymoon was over, he was sent to Washington to help the Americans build their air force, and somehow found time to write his autobiography, *Winged Warfare*.

He briefly returned to the war in April 1918, was promoted to major and given command of 85 Squadron, the "Flying Foxes." However, the Canadian military authorities, keen on organizing their own air force, were worried that Canada's most famous war hero would be killed in action. They removed him from active duty on June 19, 1918, just a few months before the war ended. He was furious at not being able to see the war through to its conclusion and, in defiance, made one final expedition on his last day. He shot down five planes, his highest single-day score, to make a total of 72 victories. He was only 24 years old at the time.

Bishop's life between the World Wars was spent on lecture tours, vacations with his wife and children (Arthur, born in 1923, and Jackie, born in 1926, both of whom eventually joined the air force) and failed business ventures, including a short-lived chartered flight company he started with fellow World War I fighter ace Billy Barker. Basically, he was a fighter pilot trying to figure out what to do with the rest of his life. He found his "niche" in 1939, when World War II broke out. The Canadian government promoted him to Honorary Air Marshal, putting him in charge of recruitment. Here, the high-profile and tireless aviator excelled. The Royal Canadian Air Force was inundated with applicants and even had to turn many away. Bishop also helped set up the Commonwealth Air Training Plan, which produced 55,000 airmen by the end of the war, making the RCAF the fourth largest allied air force.

As an acknowledgment to his important contributions to the war effort, he had a cameo role (playing himself) in the 1942 RCAF tribute film *Captains of the Clouds*, starring James Cagney. In 1944, King George VI made him a Commander of the Order of the Bath.

World War II ended on September 2, 1945, but it didn't stop Bishop from wanting to serve his country—and maybe taste the thrill of combat one last time. In 1950, at age 56, he turned quite a few heads at the RCAF when he tried to enlist for the Korean War. His application was politely refused.

William Avery Bishop died quietly in his sleep in 1956 while wintering in Palm Beach, Florida. He is buried in Greenwood Cemetery in Owen Sound, Ontario.

CHAPTER SEVEN

Sir Arthur Currie
(1875–1933)

CONFEDERATION MAY HAVE PUT CANADA on the map, but Vimy Ridge made it a nation. Before that seminal World War I offensive, Canada was a collection of provinces populated by disparate, sometimes hostile, peoples. Until then, the Canadian people had no rallying point, no unifying thread. But on that bump in the French landscape during April 1917, fighting men from all nine provinces (Newfoundland had yet to join Canada) banded together for the first time in history and gave the enemy a taste of Canadian grit. It became the greatest Allied victory of the war to that point and the first in a string of Canadian victories until the Armistice ended the war on November 11, 1918. Canada's contribution in the war bought a seat at the table of world powers, at the cost of 66,655 dead and 172,950 wounded out of a total 619,000 Canadians involved in the war effort.

Arthur Currie was the man who led the Canadian Corps—the feared "shock troops" of the British Empire—down much of the path to glory. This unlikeable, obstinate, foul-mouthed and

rather doughy-looking insurance-salesman-
turned-military-mastermind was famous for using
brains rather than his men's blood to win battles.
He became notorious for refusing to follow orders
if he didn't believe the intended goal justified the
human sacrifice. Unlike most of the war's emotionally detached leaders, he was opposed to waging a "war of attrition"—the military strategy that
most closely resembles a human meat grinder—
where each side threw thousands of soldiers at
each other until the loser ran out of cannon fod-
der. Nevertheless, he was lumped with the war's
other "butchers" by the armchair generals of his
day, including the wartime Minister of Militia and
Defence Samuel Hughes. When a newspaper in
Ontario accused him of "deliberate and useless
waste of human life," Currie went as far as suing
for libel. Not surprisingly, he won.

Arthur William Curry was born on December 5,
1875, in the farm town of Napperton, Ontario, the
second son and third child of Jane Patterson and
William Garner Curry's seven offspring. After
enduring a youth fraught with health problems, he
belatedly entered the Collegiate Institute of
Strathroy in 1889, at age 14. Despite his cloistered
childhood, he was an exceptional student, a
charismatic orator and a prolific essayist. Contrary
to his reputation in later years, he was a sociable
teen and, considering his lurid sense of humour
and physical appearance—tall at 1.83 metres (6'),

gaunt, and gawky—he was the leading practical jokester among his classmates. His parents hoped he would become a doctor or lawyer, but the hope faded when his father died in 1891, when Arthur was 16. He obtained a teaching certificate instead in 1893, but after a year of fruitless search for employment, he pulled up stakes and went to British Columbia, where he found work in Sidney and, later, Victoria. In 1897, when he was teaching in Victoria, Curry* joined a local militia regiment. In 1900, he quit teaching and became an insurance salesman. The following year, when he was 26, he married British-born Lucy Sophia Chaworth-Muster, with whom he had a son and daughter. He continued to sell insurance and, eventually, real estate until the war broke out. Luckily for Canada, the real estate market collapsed in 1913, leaving Currie under a mountain of debt and no choice but to fall back on his other source of income, the militia.

Currie's first taste of militia life came at age 22, as a gunner with the 5th Regiment (BC Brigade Canadian Garrison Artillery). In 1909, he was 34 years old, and he had become his regiment's commander, with the rank of lieutenant-colonel. In September 1913, after 16 years of dutiful militia service, Lieutenant-Colonel Currie went on leave and was planning to retire from militia service.

---

*Interestingly, he changed his last name to "Currie" around this time because his fellow militiamen kept making puns on the original spelling.

That same month, the Scottish population of Victoria was trying to mobilize its own regiment, the 50th Regiment of Foot (Gordon Highlanders of Canada), but lacked a commanding officer. When asked to take the job, Currie laughed at the notion, being neither Scottish, nor apt to look particularly sharp in a tartan kilt (the wiry frame of his youth had, by this time, surrendered to the unflattering paunch of middle-age). After some deliberation and much prodding from friends, he reluctantly took the post on January 2, 1914. The decision forever changed his life.

One of the officers he befriended in the 5th Regiment was Major Garnet Hughes, the son of his future nemesis Sam Hughes, minister of militia and defence. But in the months before the war began, the three were still on cordial terms. In fact, it was Minister Hughes who offered Currie command of the 2nd Canadian Infantry Brigade at Valcartier, Québec, and Major Hughes who convinced him to accept. Thus Currie, until then a civilian and an amateur soldier who had never commanded more than 400 militiamen, was put in charge of 4000 raw soldiers on the eve of a horrible, epic conflict.

When Currie arrived at Valcartier on September 1, 1914, the 2nd Brigade was all chaos and confusion, with no staff and little or no functioning equipment. He was given a month to assemble his command staff, establish a rapport with his officers and bring order to his troops. With a somewhat shaky foundation laid, Currie's unit left for Plymouth,

England on October 3, 1914, to begin more extensive training at Salisbury Plain, arriving on October 20. Despite the bad weather, numerous breaches of discipline and an outbreak of meningitis, Currie succeeded in producing an exemplary force, in addition to growing considerably as a leader. His rigorous methods drew uncharacteristic compliments from his British superiors, who usually frowned upon the rowdy and undisciplined Canadians, and he was promoted to colonel.

From France, the 2nd Brigade was sent to the Flanders region of Belgium to relieve the remnants of the 11th French Division and to participate in the Second Battle of Ypres. Everything looked quiet on the front line when Currie and his men arrived on the morning of April 14, 1915, but a sinister plan was being hatched in the enemy trenches.

The next day, Currie noted in his diary about a story circulating in the Allied camps that had originated from a German deserter: "Attack expected at night, to be preceded by sending of poisonous gases to our lines."

The battalions closest to the front line were warned about the alleged attack, but none of the soldiers at risk seemed to know what the part about "poisonous gases" meant. Chemical weapons had only been used once before against the Russians and only in small quantity, so no one really knew what to expect. When the right wind conditions appeared on April 22, the German released 160 tonnes of chlorine gas against French

colonial and Algerian troops, 5000 of whom died
by asphyxiation in the first 10 minutes. Most fled,
which left a 6.5-kilometre gap in the front line.
Even the Germans hadn't anticipated such effec-
tiveness and weren't able to take advantage of their
sudden victory. The 1st Canadian Division took over
the abandoned positions and received the Germans'
redoubled efforts. On April 24, besides sustaining
continuous shelling, the trench of the 2nd Brigade
and Currie's command post were enveloped in a
wall of yellow-green chlorine fog. Being heavier
than air, the ghastly, five-metre-high vapour cloud
flowed down into the trenches, burning the eyes
and lungs of all who breathed it, while machine-
gun fire took care of anyone trying to climb to
higher ground. The Canadians fought bravely
through the hellish ordeal, using urine-soaked
handkerchiefs as makeshift gas masks (the ammo-
nia in urine neutralizes chlorine).

Although the Second Battle of Ypres ended in
deadlock, the soldiers of the 1st Canadian Division
didn't budge from their stretch of front line, holding out until May 4—an unbelievable 11 days. The
18,000-strong Canadian force suffered 2000 dead
and 4000 wounded, but they had also repelled a
major military power in their first engagement in
Europe. Consequently, they received some of the
highest decorations ever awarded. For the duration of the conflict, Colonel Currie denied himself
sleep and worked the lines of communication
between his battalions and the higher command to

support his men to the fullest of his capacity. For his outstanding leadership, Britain made him a Companion of the Order of the Bath (CB), while France named him a Commander of the *Légion d'honneur* (Legion of Honour).

In September 1915, Currie was promoted to major-general and assumed command of the 1st Canadian Division from Lieutenant-General Edwin Alderson, who was made commander-in-chief of the newly created Canadian Corps. Except for a few weeks around Christmas time in 1915 with his family, Currie was consumed over the next several months with restructuring his depleted unit to make it operational again. Still, he managed to find the time to butt heads with Sam Hughes on several issues, from the horribly inadequate Canadian-issued Ross rifle, to Hughes's assertion that all British officers should be immediately removed from the Canadian Corps, and one mutually disagreeable situation, where Lieutenant-General Alderson promoted the minister's son to the command of a brigade within Currie's division.

From July 1 to November 21, 1916, the war was dominated by the bloodbath known as the Somme that resulted in a combined 2 million casualties. When the fighting began, Currie's 1st Division was still in Flanders, where, at the cost of many casualties, it had successfully recaptured Mount Sorel on June 13 after the 2nd and 3rd Canadian divisions had tried and failed. The Canadian Corps, now under the famous Lieutenant-General Sir Julian Byng, did not join in the Somme battle until its resounding victory in the Battle of Flers-Courcelette, on September 15 (Currie's 1st Division was not present). It was the most successful single day's fighting on the Somme to date, although it is now remembered chiefly for being the debut of the tank (even if the two-kilometre-an-hour mechanized turtle that became stuck in the mud was only really useful for its shock value). Major-General Currie and the remaining troops of the 1st Division arrived at the Somme front on September 22, their minds and bodies shattered from waging war in Belgium, where many of their brother officers and men now lay under fields of poppies. Before long, the mood among the first three divisions of the Canadian Corps was sombre.

In the first weeks of October, the commanders of the 1st, 2nd and 3rd Canadian divisions saw their numbers greatly reduced when, one after the other, they were ordered (in Currie's case, against vehement protestations) to have their units attack a series of well-defended German entrenchments protecting a central dugout called "Regina Trench." Each push brought them closer to their objective, but with no success. Following a heavy bombardment, the 4th Division eventually captured the sought-after trench on November 11, though by then it was merely "a depression in the chalk."

All told, the Somme cost the Canadian Corps 24,029 casualties. Yet, it was there that Canadian soldiers cultivated their reputation as the shock troops of the British Empire. According to then British Prime Minister Lloyd George: "The remainder of the way [the Canadians] were brought along to head the assault in one great battle after another. Whenever the Germans found the Canadian Corps coming into the line, they prepared for the worst." Yet, beginning in October 1916, it was Currie and his fellow generals who were the ones preparing—for victory and Vimy Ridge.

Vimy Ridge is the first time all four divisions of the Canadian Corps fought together (along with the British 5th Infantry Division) but the importance of that landmark goes beyond mere nostalgia. The ridge was a major bulwark in the Germans' Hindenburg defence line, a sunken fortress of concrete "pill-boxes," deep trenches and tunnels, coils of barbed wire a storey high and a formidable arsenal of machine-guns and heavy artillery. The French and British had already tried to take the ridge and suffered almost 200,000 dead and wounded.

Unlike their unfortunate allies, Major-General Currie and the rest of the Canadian Corps leadership under Lieutenant-General Byng had the benefit of hindsight to guide their strategies. October 1916 began a period of exhaustive preparation for the impending battle. As Lieutenant-General Byng's chief-of-staff, Currie was instrumental in the operation's painstaking coordination. Staff officers studied offensive training manuals and recent victories; troops practiced offensive movements on a life-size replica of the enemy fortifications and trenches until they became second nature; sappers (miners) dug massive tunnels under the German trenches, which they filled with explosives; and roads and light railways were built or improved to transport innumerable supplies and the hundreds of thousands of heavy artillery shells needed. Currie was especially emphatic about having each division's component units, from brigade to platoon, train to operate independently. Furthermore, every soldier was issued a map of the battleground and was intimately acquainted with his unit's objective so they could take over if their superior officer was killed.

"Thorough preparation must lead to success," Currie told his troops, "Neglect nothing."

The continuous bombardment of the enemy's fortifications began on March 20, intensifying between April 2 and 8 (more than one million shells—about 50,000 tonnes of explosives—fell on the Germans, who called that time "the week of suffering"). The employment of heavy guns and mortars at Vimy Ridge was vital to the operation's success, and skilled engineers were used to precisely locate and destroy targets.

The infantry attack was postponed because of bad weather, but it finally began at 5:30 AM on Easter Monday, April 9, when a driving wind shifted the blinding sleet and snow towards the German trenches. The Canadians charged across the muddy lunar landscape of vast shell craters, supported by almost 1000 heavy artillery and 150 machine guns.

(The bombardment was so loud it could be heard from London.) The infantrymen trailed behind a "creeping barrage," a perfectly timed artillery assault, where the shells land just ahead of the advancing troops, blowing up any barbed wire or enemy resistance in its path. The Canadians were deployed in platoons of 30 or 40—not the standard single massive flood of troops—to create smaller targets for German machine-gunners. Rushing up the slope, the first wave attacked with rifles and grenades, and when ammunition ran out, gun butts and bayonets. Just like in the rehearsals, when an officer fell, the chain of command passed down through the ranks, from lieutenant to sergeant to corporal and even private, without a hitch.

The offensive was quite literally a smash. In a few hours, the Canadians and British were the kings of the mountain, with the entire ridge in their possession, except for two sections, "Hill 145" and "the Pimple," which were captured three days later. More than one-third of the Corps' 30,000 troops became casualties, with 3598 dead and 7104 wounded. But the victory was a tremendous blow to the Germans, who considered the ridge to be impregnable. The effect was even more dramatic in the Allied camp, where gains in territory had for so long been measured in terms of metres (at the Somme, two soldiers had died for every centimetre the enemy was pushed back).

Likewise, Vimy Ridge's impact on both the war and the Canadian psyche cannot be underestimated.

It became a national point of pride and remained in Allied hands even when the Germans were poised to take Paris. Four Canadians were awarded the Victoria Cross, and for his exceptional leadership, Currie was promoted to lieutenant-general. He became the first Canadian-born commander-in-chief of the Canadian Corps on June 8, 1917. Nine days later, at Albert, France, King George V dubbed Currie a Knight Commander of the Order of St. Michael and St. George. But this was only the beginning of Sir Arthur's incredible ascendancy as one of the greatest Canadian generals of all time.

Under Currie's steady command, the Canadian Corps won victories at "Hill 70," near Arras, France, in August 1917, and Passchendaele, Belgium, later that year, earning him both a French and a Belgian *Croix de Guerre* and an induction to *l'Ordre de la Couronne* by the King of Belgium. (There would be many, many more awards.) The Corps maintained its winning record throughout the last few months of the war in 1918, known as Canada's "Hundred Days"—no small feat as the fatigue, depression, disease and frustration of several years of fighting continually gnawed at soldiers' morale.

From August 8, 1918, "the black day of the German army," to Armistice on the 11th hour of the 11th day of the 11th month, Currie led the Corps to victory upon victory. From Amiens to Cambrai, at Valenciennes and finally, Mons, Canadian troops fought side-by-side, spurred on by the memory of fallen brethren to pound the enemy into submission.

Their sacrifice brought Canada glory and honour the world over, and every year on Remembrance Day they are honoured still. Lieutenant-General Sir Arthur Currie, KCB, KCMG, etc., was given a hero's welcome in London, where he led the Canadian Corps in their victory parade.

His homecoming, on the other hand, was no more than lukewarm at best, due mainly to ex-minister of militia and defence Sam Hughes and his clique on Parliament Hill fomenting the belief that Currie had uncaringly led Canadian soldiers to the slaughter. Sadly, many citizens, weary of the war and all its horrors, bought this patent falsehood. Although Currie didn't show emotion, the slur wounded him deeper than any bullet ever could. Currie was appointed to inspector-general of Canada's military in 1919, though his best efforts could not win over his opponents in Ottawa. In June 1920, he accepted the position of principal and vice-chancellor at McGill University, where he presided over the venerable institution's single greatest period of expansion for 13 years.

In 1927, a notorious newspaper editorial accusing him of "butchery" was published in a small Ontario newspaper, *The Port Hope Guide*, sparking the famous Currie libel trial. He finally vindicated himself in 1928, but the strain exacted a heavy toll on his health. Sir Arthur died five years later on November 30, 1933, at age 58. He is buried at Mont Royal Cemetery in Montréal.

CHAPTER EIGHT

Georges-Philéas Vanier
(1888–1967)

LIKE MANY YOUNG MEN OF HIS DAY, Georges Vanier held an idealistic world view when he enlisted to serve his country in World War I. The reality was much less romantic—friends killed by the dozens, countrymen by the thousands. He even lost a leg in the fighting. Yet, despite the lifelong pain he endured from his bodily wounds, the war failed to scar his psyche. Instead, it transformed the decorated veteran into a more spiritual and compassionate human being, eager to help the have-nots of the world. With the help of his like-minded wife, he carried the heroic spirit of his military days into every other vocation of his lifelong service to our country, whether as a diplomat, governor general or humanitarian. In 1998, *Maclean's* magazine ranked him number one on their "Top 100 People of the Century" list, and the Catholic Church has nominated him and his wife for beatification, the first step towards official sainthood. Although it is doubtful he will ever be canonized, it is true that few Canadians have devoted as much of themselves to raising the noble spirit of this proud nation—whether Anglo or francophone, rich or poor, First Nation or newly-landed immigrant—than Georges Vanier.

Georges-Philéas Vanier was born on April 23, 1888, in Montréal, Québec, to Irish-born Margaret Maloney, and Philéas Vanier, a well-heeled Montréal realtor of old French-Canadian stock. Interestingly, though he is considered one of the most prominent French-Canadians in the nation's history, Georges and his four younger siblings grew up in an English-speaking household. Their mother didn't speak much French and their father thought it good practice for his business dealings with Anglophones. Likewise, he attended an English school, the prestigious Jesuit-run Loyola College beginning in 1897 at age nine. He graduated at the top of his class with a Bachelor of Arts in 1906 when he was 18. A studious and somewhat overly serious young man, Georges was an avid reader of classical English literature and a fixture at downtown Montréal's used bookstores—the tall, robust lad was as much a sports fanatic as he was a bookworm. But, despite the Anglo trappings of his childhood and adolescence, Georges maintained a deep connection to his French-Canadian roots and *la francophonie* in general, spurring him to learn the language, history and literature of Molière, de Balzac and Rousseau. As a result, he acquired a lifelong love of France while still in his late teens, though the romance would take some very unexpected twists.

After a few months of deliberation on whether to join the priesthood, the ex-Catholic schoolboy opted to study law instead at l'Université de Laval. He graduated in the summer of 1911, but before joining the bar, he decided to take some time off to visit the major cities and sites of southern Ontario and the neighbouring regions of the U.S. A few months later, in February 1912, Vanier boarded the aptly named S.S. *Franconia* for his first tour of Europe, visiting all the requisite tourist destinations in France, Belgium, Germany, Italy, Ireland and England.

By the beginning of 1913, Vanier was back in Montréal and practicing law at the firm of Charles Casgrain, who urged Vanier to accept a lieutenancy that had been arranged for him in the 6th Brigade, Canadian Field Artillery. Vanier politely demurred. Barring a few scuffles in his Loyola days, he wasn't interested in fighting, but that attitude quickly changed when World War I erupted in August of 1914. Soon afterward, a group of influential Francophones got together and asked Prime Minister Sir Robert Borden for permission to recruit a regiment composed exclusively of French-Canadians. It would eventually be known as the Royal 22e Régiment, the famous "Van Doos" (a corruption of the French "*vignt-deuxième*").

Vanier was actually one of the regiment's recruiters and duly responded to the call to arms himself on November 11, 1914, enlisting with the rank of lieutenant. He was still just as pacific-minded as ever, but in a letter to his sister Frances, he intimated how he could not tolerate blithely sitting on the fence: "During the last months of 1914, I could not read the accounts of Belgian sufferings without feeling a deep compassion and an active desire to right, as far as it was in my power, the heinous wrongs done."

The 1100-strong Van Doos departed from Halifax on May 20, 1915, reaching Devonport, England, on May 29. At East Sandling Camp, near the English Channel coast, Georges learned how to read maps, fire a machine gun and use a bayonet, and the whole regiment rehearsed trench warfare scenarios. Yet, all the play fighting in the world failed to prepare the Van Doos for the awful reality of the next three years, during which time the regiment suffered a 64-percent casualty rate. Training continued unabated until September 1915, when the Van Doos crossed the Channel to Le Havre, France. The locals were apparently quite baffled at encountering French-speaking "British" soldiers—they knew little of Canada and even less about the large numbers of Francophones living there. (At one point, the regiment was even sent an interpreter!)

They arrived on September 20, 1915, at the Flemish town of Scherpenberg, Belgium, to relieve the Yorkshire Light Infantry and receive their initiation to life on the frontline, just 75 to 100 metres from the enemy trenches—close enough to make death by sniper fire or grenades an almost routine occurrence. Like most novices to the war, Vanier

optimistically predicted: "after 12 months of hard-
ship and privation, the old-time dash of the most
gallant of nations will carry us through—and we
are *going* through." Two months later, when the
early November rains turned the landscape into a
sea of brown sludge, he was already singing a more
melancholy tune: "A dismal morning; low clouds;
everything is heavy…appropriate conditions for
the month of the Dead."

On January 2, 1916, Vanier led a small demoli-
tions team of five men on a night operation—the
capture and destruction of a ramshackle hut near
the German lines that was suspected of being an
enemy machine gun emplacement. Crawling much
of the way over the frozen ground on their bellies
and forced to cut through several lines of barbed
wire while bullets zinged overhead, Lieutenant
Vanier's team managed to make it to the hut and
back without incident in under an hour.

For the stealth and speed of the operation, Vanier
was promoted to captain and later awarded a Military Cross and a French *Légion d'honneur*. However,
on June 9, 1916, before he could receive his
medals, he was nearly killed by a shell that
exploded a few feet away from him. The resulting
shell shock sent him to England for the next four
months to recover. Fortunately, his sick leave coincided with the Battle of Courcelette, the bloody
affair that claimed so many of his friends' lives that
he hardly recognized his regiment when he
returned to the front on August 9, 1916.

A year later, in August 1917, Captain Vanier and the Van Doos saw many more casualties during the victorious fighting at Hill 70 (near Lens, France) and later in November at Passchendaele, Flanders. To get to the front line of the bombed-out wasteland that was Passchendaele, the Van Doos had to negotiate a narrow, semi-liquefied trench more than 10 kilometres long while being steadily assaulted by German artillery. One of Vanier's fellow officers, Capt. Henri Chassé, later described one of the unique miseries of that walk:

> We were forced to follow [the trench] as best we could, although in certain places it was partially demolished, and you risked death by submersion in the mud if you put your foot to one side. Unfortunately, a number of our comrades met their end in this horrible way.

The price of the German defeat was 16,000 killed or wounded Canadians during two weeks of fighting. The British and Australian forces had fought for almost four months without budging the Germans, at a cost of over 100,000 casualties.

August 1918 began Canada's "Hundred Days," when the Canadian Corps led the charge to the French city of Mons, leaving a trail of captured or destroyed German positions in its wake. Yet, even with the Allies on the cusp of shattering the Hindenburg line of defence, the Germans kept up an unrelenting firefight to the very end. During August 1918, the Van Doos fought a series of battles between Arras and Cambrai. One of these conflicts took place at a small town called Chérisy, where the regiment was nearly wiped out, and Vanier himself just barely made it out alive. Years later, he described the life-altering moment, in an interview on CBC radio:

> At 10:00 AM, our artillery opened an intense bar-rage on all the German positions. A few minutes later the 22nd went over the top. They were met with intense fire and until noon, they advanced slowly in small groups, from shell hole to shell hole, crossing barbed wire in the face of heavy fire, particularly from machine guns. During the attack, Lieutenant-Colonel Antoine Dubuc…was struck in the eye by a bullet…General Tremblay ordered me up to take command of the remnants—and they were literally remnants! When I reached the battalion at dusk, the troops were all scattered in shell holes, without any definite trench line…. At about 9:30 the next morn-ing, the 28th of August, a staff officer arrived with the news that our two battalions would be attacking again at 12:30 PM that day…. As the men were scat-tered and in full view, except for the cover the shell holes could furnish, it wasn't possible to make any ideal distribution before the attack. I called a meeting in a large shell hole of the few officers who were left. I told them about the new attack, and in the circum-stances, there was only one thing to do, when the bar-rage fell the officers were to rise and call on the men to follow, and that is what happened. But, we didn't get very far. [Our artillery] barrage was not a heavy one and there were many enemy machine guns.

The tall captain was an easy target at the head of the suicidal charge, and an enemy machine-gunner shot Vanier clean through the chest. Fortunately, the bullet missed his spine by centimetres, but he wasn't yet out of danger. A stretcher bearer was hastily bandaging-up his wound when a heavy shell landed a few feet away, tearing the stretcher bearer apart and lacing both Vanier's legs with shrapnel. Bleeding profusely and in agonizing pain, he was rushed to a casualty clearing station, where he was told that his right knee was splintered to pieces, and his leg should be amputated. Vanier asked to be able to sleep on the decision, although considering the circumstances, it's doubtful he could have slept much. The following day, on August 28, the leg was amputated just above the knee, ending his active military career at age 30, just two and a half months shy of the armistice.

Despite the heavy losses, the High Command praised Vanier's leadership and his men's dauntless courage in facilitating the capture of Chérisy, as well as the Allied advance.

Vanier underwent two more operations in England, spending several months there recuperating and learning how to walk with an artificial limb. On May 27, 1919, a Bar was added to his Military Cross, and he was also awarded a Distinguished Service Order by King George V at Buckingham Palace.

By the end of July 1919, Vanier was back in Québec, enjoying some peace and quiet at his family's

chalet on Lake Memphremagog while he decided
what to do with himself. He could have returned
to law, but his beloved Van Doos—now a permanent unit housed at the Citadel of Québec City—
were much closer to his heart. Canada's new
inspector-general, Sir Arthur Currie, questioned
the usefulness of an officer with only one leg, but
eventually permitted Vanier (now a major) to
rejoin the regiment as second-in-command. Not
long after, while meeting his old commanding
officer, Major-General Tremblay, for lunch at
Montréal's Ritz-Carlton Hotel, he was introduced
to his future wife and mother of his five children.

The two had much in common. Like Vanier,
22-year-old Pauline Archer was tall, thin and from
a well-to-do family with some British ancestry. Also,
like her future groom, she was a deeply religious
woman with a tender heart, especially for the less
fortunate of the world. Although Vanier was so inept
with women that he almost lost Pauline to another
suitor, he finally worked up the nerve to propose to
her, and they were married on September 7, 1921
at the Notre-Dame Basilica in Montréal. The occa-
sion was momentous enough, if only for rousing
the 33-year-old Vanier from his hermitic lifestyle,
but it also opened a whole new chapter on his
post-war life.

When Lord Byng of Vimy was appointed Governor
General of Canada in August 1921, he decided to
appoint a French-Canadian as his aide-de-camp and
chose Vanier for the job. The Byngs and the Vaniers

became close friends, sharing a passion for hockey, to which the Lady Byng Trophy owes its name. Lord Byng knew of Vanier's desire to move up in the military ranks, so he helped secure Georges' entrance into the prestigious officers' college in Camberley, England. Upon his return to Canada in 1925, Vanier became the Royal 22e Regiment's commanding officer. In February 1928, he joined the Canadian military delegation for disarmament to the League of Nations in Geneva, Switzerland, thereby beginning his diplomatic career.

Throughout most of the 1930s, Vanier held various positions in London, representing Canada at the War Graves Commission, the League of Nations Assembly and the coronation of George VI, among others. In December 1938, a month after the *Kristallnacht* in Germany, he entered a turbulent period in both his life and Canada's history when he was appointed Minister of the Legation in Paris.

Germany began yet another cycle of worldwide aggression on September 1, 1939, when it invaded Poland. By May 1940, the bombing of Paris had begun, and like thousands of other refugees, Pauline was forced to flee with her children to London, where she joined the Red Cross. This harrowing experience no doubt influenced Pauline (and by extension, her husband) to empathize with the plight of refugees.

Vanier became outspoken about the Germans' cruelty and wanton murder after seeking refuge in London, and he and Pauline continued to openly discuss Nazi war crimes (though they were not yet called that) when they returned to Canada the following year, in 1941. Perhaps foreseeing the horrors yet to come, they entreated Mackenzie King's government to relax immigration policies and open the door to Europe's refugees—especially the Jews, who seemed to be a favourite target of the Nazis. Unfortunately, xenophobia and anti-Semitism were the rules of the day, and only about 5000 Jews were allowed into the country during the entire 12 years of the Nazi regime (the U.S. accepted 200,000 and even China took in about 25,000).

At the beginning of 1943, the Vaniers returned to London, where Georges was declared the ambassador to several German-occupied countries. In mid-1943, Georges and Pauline moved once again, this time to Algiers, Algeria, where they lent their support to General Charles de Gaulle's French Committee of National Liberation.

The Vaniers returned to Paris following its liberation on August 25, 1944, and Georges redoubled his efforts to open the hearts of Canada's politicians to the poor refugees who kept showing up at his doorstep. While her husband's pleas fell on deaf ears, Pauline took matters into her own hands, organizing an impromptu help centre at Paris's train station:

> *We greeted the refugees with drinks, refreshments, clothes and survival kits, and tried to reach their families, friends or anyone who might take them in. Many, however, had no idea whether*

anyone they knew was still alive, let alone their
whereabouts. For them, we arranged temporary
shelter. Then we took their photos and stuck these
up on long panels lining both sides of the railway
station in hopes that someone in the crowds
would recognize the name or the picture of a long-
lost relative or friend.

Vanier visited the Buchenwald concentration
camp with several American congressmen in
April 1945 just after it was liberated. The abomi-
nations he found there—skeletal inmates, death
chambers and one grisly lampshade made of
human skin— saddened him to his very soul. He
subsequently made an impassioned speech,
broadcast across Canada by CBC radio, that put
into words the disgrace of the nation's indifference: "How deaf we were then, to cruelty and the
cries of pain which came to our ears, grim fore-
runners of the mass torture and murders which
were to follow." Only after the war had ended did
Canada open its border, accepting almost 200,000
refugees between 1947 and 1953.

In 1953, at age 65, Vanier retired from diplomatic service and settled down with his wife in
Montréal, though they didn't slow down. In 1959,
when he was 71 years old, Vanier became the first
French-Canadian governor general in history. His
appointment came at a time of economic uncer-
tainty, successive minority governments and rising
Québec nationalism. In addition, Vanier had
developed a heart condition and, consequently,

was in poor health. Nevertheless, Georges and Pauline criss-crossed the country to raise the pro-file of issues that concerned them, such as poverty, youth and family well-being, and national unity.

After suffering a heart attack in 1966, Vanier's health declined rapidly, and only his indomitable will allowed him to meet his many obligations. He knew his time was running out. The morning of March 5, 1967, he and Pauline attended a pri-vate mass at Rideau Hall. He died of heart failure a few hours later at the age of 79. His remains are entombed in the commemorative chapel at the Citadel in Québec City.

Some of the many legacies Georges Vanier left behind are the Vanier Awards for Outstanding Young Canadians, the Vanier Cup for the national university football championship and the Vanier Institute of the Family. The Vaniers also passed on their benevolent spirit to their son Jean, a famous humanitarian in his own right. In 1964, he co-founded *L'Arche* in Trosly-Breuil, France, now a worldwide organization of 124 communities that aims to "bring together people with a learning disability and those who choose to share their lives by living in the same home, and sharing the same workplace." After her husband's death, Pauline Vanier joined her son in France. She died there in 1991, at the age of 93.

CHAPTER NINE

Roméo Dallaire
(1945–)

If the United Nations were effective as a security agency—which it is not—these limited [peacekeeping] arrangements would be unnecessary and, therefore, undesirable. But pending that day, can we not put some force behind the United Nations which, under the authorization of the Assembly, might be useful at least for dealing with some small conflicts and preventing them from becoming great ones?

–Former Prime Minister Lester B. Pearson's 1957 Nobel Peace Prize acceptance speech

IN 1957, WHEN THE SUEZ CANAL CRISIS in Egypt threatened to escalate into "World War III," a Canadian diplomat named Lester B. Pearson proposed that a lightly armed, impartial and multinational coalition of soldiers be sent to defuse the situation. His recommendations led to the creation of the United Nations Emergency Force (UNEF) and the birth of international peacekeeping as we know it. Pearson inadvertently changed the face of Canada's military (arguably for the worse) and established what has become a revered Canadian tradition, as much a part of Canada's national military culture as hockey is to sports or "free" is to health care. Canada is rightly proud of the more than 100,000 Canadian soldiers who have been involved in more than 50 UN peacekeeping missions around the world, 107 of whom have lost their lives in the name of peace.

However, Canada's commitment to Pearsonian do-goodism has been on the wane for more than a decade. A major factor for its decline is the series of colossal UN fiascos that occurred in the early 1990s—involving Canadian soldiers—that severely damaged the reputations of both peacekeeping and the UN. The Rwandan Genocide is perhaps one of the worst examples of the international community's failure to intervene in a man-made disaster.

From 1993 to 1994, Major-General Roméo Dallaire commanded the UN Assistance Mission for Rwanda (UNAMIR) that was at the scene of one of humanity's worst crimes—the brutal slaughter of over 800,000 men, women and children and the subsequent displacement of two million refugees. Although he has since been praised for his courage and leadership, many blame him for instilling a sense of false security in the victims of the Rwandan Genocide by his, and the UN's, very presence. Yet, like the people of Rwanda, Dallaire never imagined that the world could be so callous, that it would abandon an entire people in their darkest hour. With proper support, he could have prevented some, if not all, of the bloodshed, but the world's leaders didn't care about the people of that tiny, backward African nation of no real strategic or economic importance. Despite a lack of support and in the face of incredible danger, Dallaire did everything he could to help the people of Rwanda and is credited with saving at least 30,000 people from certain death, though the memories of Rwanda will haunt him forever.

Romualdus Antonius Johannes Loudivicus Roméo Dallaire was born on June 25, 1946, in Denekamp, Holland. His father, Canadian Staff-Sergeant Roméo Louis Dallaire, had stayed behind in Holland after World War II to redeploy leftover munitions. Roméo senior met a young Dutch nurse named Catherine Johanna Vermeassen while lodging with a local family. They were soon married in 1945, and Roméo junior—with a name fit for a Roman general—was born shortly thereafter.

The future Major-General Dallaire grew up in a working-class, mainly Francophone neighbourhood in east-end Montréal, although he spoke both English and French at home. Despite his father's warning that French-Canadians don't get very far in the army, Dallaire was determined to become a military man like his dad. Already a Boy Scout from a young age, he joined the Canadian Army Cadets when he was 14, the Reserves at 16, and in 1964 when he was 18 years old, he enrolled at *Le Collège militaire royal de Saint-Jean*, in St. Jean, Québec. Dallaire went on to the Royal Military College of Kingston, Ontario, where he graduated with a Bachelor of Science degree in 1969. He continued taking officer courses in the 1970s, in between serving at various bases in Canada and the NATO base in Lahr, West Germany. It was during this time, while garrisoned in Québec, that he met Elizabeth Roberge, also the child of a World War II veteran, whom he married in 1976 and with whom he has had three children— Willem, Catherine and Guy.

Throughout the 1980s, Dallaire was employed in various capacities in the Canadian Forces. From 1983 to 1985, he commanded the 5th Light Artillery Regiment, in Valcartier, Québec. In 1986, after receiving a promotion to colonel, he assumed the directorships of both the Land Forces Requirements and Artillery departments in Ottawa. He experienced a great moment of pride on July 3, 1989, when he was promoted to brigadier-general and appointed commander of his *alma mater* in St.-Jean. Finally, in the summer of 1991, he took over the 5th Mechanized Brigade Group at Valcartier and remained there until 1993, when he received the fateful call to report to UN Headquarters in New York City. Dallaire, one of Canada's most highly-credentialed French-Canadian generals, had been handpicked by Secretary-General Boutros Boutros-Ghali to head up the UN Observer Mission—Uganda and Rwanda (UNOMUR)—the precursor to UNAMIR.

The lean years of his childhood had shaped Dallaire into a self-motivated, workaholic officer, who was tough on his men and even tougher on himself, and it showed in the rising arc of his career. For him, the appointment was the culmination of all the hard work that had preceded it. Understandably, he jumped at the chance to lead his first big UN assignment as a peace observer in an exotic locale like Rwanda. Little did he know that all he would be observing was a bloodbath—one that he would be powerless to stop.

When Dallaire arrived in the Rwandan capital city of Kigali on October 22, 1993, amidst relative peace between the country's Hutu majority and Tutsi minority ethnic groups, he was largely ignorant of both Rwanda and the turbulent history of the nation's two main ethnic peoples. Traditionally, a Tutsi royal family had ruled Rwanda, though most of their subjects had been equally poor, regardless of ethnicity. When Europeans, particularly the Belgians, colonized the region, the Tutsi were regarded as superior to the Hutu, particularly because the generally taller, lighter-skinned, and thinner-nosed Tutsi were presumed to have descended from Christian Ethiopians, regarded as the "Caucasians of Africa." All positions of power that were not held by the Europeans were placed in Tutsi hands, causing much resentment among the Hutu.

When Rwanda achieved independence in 1962, a nationalist Hutu party took over indefinitely. A predictable backlash of reverse-racism occurred, with successive Hutu dictators calling for the "foreign" Tutsi to be sent "back to where they came from." Every few decades, tens of thousands of Tutsi were killed in reoccurring pogroms and, by 1990, hundreds of thousands of Tutsi refugees had fled Rwanda. A large exile community formed in neighbouring Uganda, where a Tutsi rebel leader named Paul Kagame had started the Rwandanese Patriotic Front (RPF) in 1985, with the aim of overthrowing the oppressive Hutu government and securing his people's return to their homeland.

In 1990, the RPF invaded Rwanda, and fighting between the rebel and government forces continued for almost two years. Finally, in July 1992, a ceasefire was declared. After several months of negotiations between Kagame and Rwanda's Hutu dictator, General Juvénal Habyarimana, the last phase of the historic Arusha Accords was signed on August 4, 1993, ostensibly creating peace, albeit fragile, between the belligerent parties. The crux of the Accords was the creation of a Hutu-Tutsi transitional government until democratic elections could be held, and the purpose of UNAMIR was to oversee its peaceful implementation without taking any sides.

At the outset, Dallaire believed that the UN's presence would be enough to discourage any violence by the Hutu regime. After all, it was the Hutu-led government that had invited the UN observers in the first place. He had no way of knowing that the state-run media had been fuelling hatred against Rwanda's Tutsi, referred to in broadcasts as the *"inyenzi"* or cockroaches. Nor was he aware of the arming of hundreds of thousands of militiamen by extremist elements within the government and military in preparation for the caustically-named "Operation Zero" (signifying how many Tutsi were to be left when they reached their objective). It wasn't long before moderate Hutu politicians, judged too sympathetic to the Tutsi, began disappearing, and Habyarimana tightened his grip on the reins of power.

As soon as Dallaire caught wind of the president's duplicity, he fired off a series of strongly worded reports to his superiors at the UN's Department of Peacekeeping Operations (DPKO), then headed by current secretary-general, Kofi Annan. Dallaire repeatedly requested additional troops, supplies and a clear mandate to use preventive force to stop bloodshed. Unfortunately, the U.S.—the true muscle behind the UN—had just endured the Black Hawk Down incident in Somalia, where 18 of its soldiers had died. Consequently, the Americans did not have the political will to relive the same horrors in another African backwater, and neither did most of the other industrialized nations (France was actually the Rwandan government's main supporter and arms dealer, and continued to be so, well into the genocide).

Even at the height of the Hutu killing spree, the UN would not refer to what was going on in Rwanda as "genocide," thereby sidestepping the moral and legal obligation to act. When Dallaire presented his minders at the DPKO with insider information stating, among other things, that the

Habyarimana government was hoarding large caches of weapons with the intention of eradicating Rwanda's Tutsi population, he was told *not* to take pre-emptive measures. The rationale was that it might give the impression that the UN was biased in favour of the Tutsi and that "the overriding consideration [of the mission] is the need to avoid entering into a course of action that might lead to the use of force and unanticipated repercussions."

The situation came to a head on April 6, 1994, when a plane carrying President Habyarimana and the Hutu president of Burundi was shot down over Kigali airport. (Militant Hutu government officials claimed it was an RPF assassination, though many believe he was taken out of the picture by power-hungry members within his own cabal.) What followed was a methodical slaughter with a purposeful intensity rivalling that of the Nazis. The *cadaveri eccellenti* began to pile up, notably those of the prime minister and the presiding judge of the constitutional court; thousands of crazed and depraved Hutu militiamen took over the city of Kigali; and orchestrated anarchy slowly spread its tentacles across Rwanda.

Between April and June 1994, an estimated 800,000 to almost one million men, women and children were killed and half a million wounded. They were shot, bludgeoned and butchered with machetes, sometimes by trained army and militia members, but more often than not, by people who had been their friends, neighbours, even clergymen.

The brutality was stunning—Dallaire later told a reporter of an incident witnessed by one of his officers of "a crowd encouraging a girl of 14 or 15 with a machete and a child on her back to kill another girl of 14 or 15 with a child on her back" and the crowd cheering when one chopped the other to death. Many survivors would later recount how they lost 30 or 40 of their relatives in a single day. Far too many families have no survivors left to tell their tale.

Incredibly, the genocide was so widespread and had so many participants that the entire event unfolded within the span of a mere 100 days. Yet, while images of dismembered bodies floating down the Nile River flashed on television screens around the world, and the UN was inundated with pleas from humanitarian organizations and its own personnel to do something, the world's leaders kept their heads buried deep in the sand.

Sadly, in the middle of all the confusion on April 7, a group of 10 Belgian peacekeepers were captured, tortured and killed. Public backlash in Belgium at Dallaire's failure to protect these men caused Brussels to pull its remaining 440 soldiers out of UNAMIR, depriving the mission of its best troops. The irony was not lost on Dallaire: "Fifty years earlier, my father was fighting through Belgium with the Allies. And there I was in an ex-colony of Belgium—the country that had created some of the problems we were facing there—and right at the worst time the Belgians were packing up and leaving a Canadian to defend himself."

The Belgian withdrawal was only the first of many, as most of the 24 other countries in the UNAMIR coalition followed suit. Dallaire's already paltry force of 2548 soldiers was further whittled down to himself, Ghanaian brigadier-general Henry Anyidoho, Canadian Major Brent Beardsley and 450 troops—all from African nations.

Less than a week after the genocide began, Dallaire saw the writing on the wall. On April 12, he cabled New York with a request that UNAMIR's mandate be changed. He wanted a 5000-strong rapid reaction force of proper soldiers (no more Third World cast-offs to boost the participation numbers) and wanted permission to go into Kigali with guns blazing to create a "safe zone" for persecuted Rwandans. It was the only thing that could slow down the *genocidaires'* killing machine, but it was the last thing that the UN powerbrokers wanted. In fact, they wanted to pull the plug on the mission as soon as all foreign nationals were evacuated and tried to downplay the genocide, even parroting the Rwandan government's line that it was simply "self-defence" against Paul Kagame's invading RPF forces.

Nevertheless, Dallaire pressed on and concentrated his remaining force around a handful of small "safe zones" in Kigali, as well as the capital's airport. After some pleading, the Canadian government agreed to fly humanitarian aid and aid workers

from the Red Cross and *Médecins Sans Frontières* into
Rwanda and, when possible, sneak some refugees
out. Ottawa also changed its tune of not wanting to
send any more soldiers to the Rwandan quagmire,
and delivered to Dallaire a dozen officers—not the
battalion he had originally asked for, but better than
nothing. Another benefit of having two relief flights
a day was that it increased the number of journalists
travelling into the country. In many respects, they
were Dallaire's most powerful weapon against UN
intransigence, though his attempt to shame the
world into action only really took effect after most
of the fighting was over.

In the meantime, he received death threats from
the Hutu forces on a regular basis, and a staff
member of UNAMIR was allegedly hired to assassinate him. But he never stopped trying to do everything in his power to protect the innocent. His
efforts are credited with directly saving at least
30,000 Tutsi from certain death. If for nothing else
in this despicable mission, it is for these actions
that he was awarded the Meritorious Service Cross
on May 20, 1994.

That same month, public awareness of the situation in Rwanda had reached critical mass, and the UN
Security Council was forced to admit to the genocide
that was taking place. On June 8, UNAMIR II was
ratified, providing a 5500-strong force from various
African countries, as well as 50 armoured personnel
carriers (APCs) and a further 2500 troops contributed by the U.S. However, all but 300 of the

American troops were to be kept in Uganda and the Democratic Republic of Congo, and both the soldiers and APCs (without radios or mounted guns) started arriving only *after* July 4, when the RPF had taken Kigali, thus ending the genocide and the war.

An estimated two million Hutu escaped the wrath of the victorious Tutsi rebels into the Democratic Republic of Congo, Burundi and Uganda—an untold number of whom were murderers trying to escape vengeful justice. On July 19, a new multi-ethnic government was created, with a Hutu president (though Tutsi members of the RPF retained most political control), and refugees were encouraged to return to Rwanda. Over a million have done so since then.

UNAMIR II remained active in the country, especially in assisting with the enormous amount of humanitarian relief (mainly from the U.S.) that came pouring into Rwanda after the RPF victory, until March 8, 1996. Dallaire, however, wasn't able to see the mission through to the end. Understandably, the effect of living through "hell on earth" proved mentally and emotionally overwhelming, and Canadian Major-General Guy Tousignant replaced him as force commander.

Upon returning to Canada, Dallaire tried to return to a normal life, and on the surface, it seemed like he was succeeding. His star kept rising. He became commander of Land Forces Québec Area, and he then held several positions within the Department of National Defence in

Ottawa, but inside he was a shambles. On April 22, 2000, Dallaire received his long-overdue medical release from the Canadian Armed Forces. Since then, he has been candid about his ordeals with post-traumatic stress disorder and serious clinical depression, including numerous suicide attempts during and after Rwanda. He has become a leading advocate for better understanding and treatment of mood disorders within the armed forces.

For his service to Canada, he was awarded the Vimy Award, the U.S. Legion of Merit Medal and honorary doctorates from several Canadian universities. In 2002 he was made an Officer of the Order of Canada.

Dallaire's chronicle of his experiences in Rwanda, *Shake Hands with the Devil: The Failure of Humanity in Rwanda*, was published in 2003. In 2004 it won the Shaughnessy Cohen Award for Political Writing and the Governor General's Award for non-fiction.

In April 2004, Dallaire exorcised some of his demons when he testified against Colonel Théoneste Bagosora, one of the alleged masterminds of the genocide, at the International Criminal Tribunal for Rwanda, based in Arusha, Tanzania. Many of the genocide's presumed conspirators are still at large.

Dallaire currently divides his time between spending time with his family and supporting various humanitarian causes.

CHAPTER TEN

Princess Patricia's Canadian Light Infantry

It's been a tough learning curve for the last 15 years. The Canadian army was optimized for a conventional war against a conventional foe. We have had to learn to change how we fight through some hard experiences....A big portion of it is making do with what you have, but in the end, it takes intellectual agility and ingenuity to do more with less. That also allows you to deal with complex situations better than armies with an abundance of resources. Having established a culture of creativity within your army, you can then take advantage of it and use it to solve complex problems in a modern environment.

– Lieutenant-Colonel Shane Schreiber, Princess Patricia's Canadian Light Infantry, 12/20/04

FROM THE WAR OF 1812 TO THE War on Terrorism, Canadian soldiers have a reputation for fighting "above their weight." Time and again, Canada's small, often underfunded, forces have taken on bigger, stronger foes and walked shoulder to shoulder into battle with much more powerful allies. Time and again, Canada's soldiers have proven, to both adversaries and allies, that strength comes not only in manpower or armaments but also in "heart"—that indelible spirit of perseverance among Canadian soldiers, often outnumbered and outgunned, but never outperformed. Even with all the changes that Canada's military has undergone since the Cold War ended, this legacy of steadfast courage can still be found in the hearts of 60,000 overworked and underappreciated Canadian military men and women.

As in other long-standing units like the Royal Canadian and "Van Doos" regiments, the troops of Princess Patricia's Canadian Light Infantry Regiment continue to uphold the best traditions of Canada's military as it enters the latest age of warfare—the War on Terrorism. For 90 years, the PPCLI or "Patricia's," has received over two dozen battle honours and individual members have received numerous accolades for their heroic exploits, while serving in disparate places around the world—Flanders, France, Korea, the Balkans and, since early 2002, in the rugged mountains of Afghanistan. This most recent site of conflict was where several of the regiment's top-notch snipers won worldwide acclaim while hunting Taliban and Al-Qaeda members in 2002. It is also where four members of the 3rd Battalion PPCLI—Sergeant Marc Léger, Corporal Ainsworth Dyer, Private Richard Green, and Private Nathan Smith—were killed in a now notorious "friendly fire" incident.

Although it is only one of the many illustrious regiments of the Canadian Forces, the Princess Patricia's Canadian Light Infantry is a shining example of why Canadians should be proud of the men and women who have risked their lives in the past and continue to do so today. Their sacrifices afford Canadians all the joys and freedoms taken for granted and, for this, it is only fitting to consider them collectively as Canadian heroes.

The Princess Patricia's Canadian Light Infantry Regiment was founded on August 6, 1914, by Captain Andrew Hamilton Gault, a wealthy Montréal businessman and Boer War veteran. When the great armies of Europe began to stir once again, following the assassination of Austro-Hungarian Archduke Franz Ferdinand, Gault foresaw the war that was about to engulf Europe and decided to create an army unit that could mobilize quickly when the hostilities commenced.

At the beginning of August 1914, he went to Ottawa to meet with the minister of militia and defence, Sam Hughes and offered to raise and equip a light cavalry regiment with $100,000 of his own money. Hughes was impressed, though he argued that if a unit were to be raised, it should be an infantry regiment.

On August 4, 1914, Germany invaded Belgium, forcing Britain to declare war and thus drawing

PRINCESS PATRICIA'S CANADIAN LIGHT INFANTRY   133

the armies of Canada and other former colonies into the fray along with it. Canada's governor general, the Duke of Connaught, approved Gault's generous proposal soon after, and as a show of gratitude, Gault named the regiment after his daughter, Princess Patricia of Connaught.

The regiment held its first parade on August 23, culminating with the presentation of the regiment's Camp Colour by Princess Patricia. She had designed the flag herself, with her intertwined initials "VP" (for Victoria Patricia) in gold on a blue centre with a crimson background. It was fastened to a branch cut from a maple tree on Parliament Hill, and the "Ric-A-Dam-Doo," as it was later called, was carried into every battle the Patricia's fought in during World War I.

The Patricia's landed in France with the 27th Division on December 20, 1914, making it the first and only Canadian fighting unit on the continent that year. On January 5, 1915, the PPCLI reached Ypres and immediately were confronted with life in the front-line trenches during winter. According to one soldier:

> It was impossible to move in or out of the trenches in daylight. They were mere ditches dug across a sea of mud, too wide to provide protection from shellfire and too shallow to be bullet-proof. In places, a man would be waist deep in water if he were to stand in the bottom of the trench. They could not be drained, hence, they could not be deepened. The walls collapsed from

*lack of revetting. There were no sandbags with
which to build a proper parapet. Unburied bodies lay both in front and behind them, and the
area was infested with rats.*

One of the Patricia's great battles, the Battle
of Frezenberg, was fought on May 8, 1915, at
Bellewaerde Lake in Belgium. Already suffering
from exhaustion and numerous casualties, forced
to use ditches and shell holes for cover and under
withering fire from three sides, the 80th Brigade
to which the PPCLI was attached was subjected to
a massive German poison gas attack. Almost the
entire original regiment was killed, and only 154
men walked away alive after the two-day
onslaught. Yet despite the death and despair that
engulfed it, the Patricia's successfully held on to the
front, earning the regiment its third battle honour.

Several prestigious decorations for gallantry
were awarded to individual members of the regiment, adding to the regiment's renown during
the Great War. Most prominent of these were the
Victoria Crosses won by Lieutenant Hugh
McKenzie and Sergeant George Harry Mullin
during the Battle of Passchendaele on October 30,
1917, and Sergeant Robert Spall at Parvillers,
France, in August, 1918.

After the Armistice, the regiment was selected
to form part of Canada's peacetime army—the
Permanent Active Militia, or Permanent Force—
on March 10, 1919. During the inter-war years,
the Canadian military was deeply affected by the

political fallout of the First World War's waste of human life, and the Patricia's were no exception. In this time of drastically diminished military spending, the regiment was reduced to 209 soldiers and officers combined, concentrated at Sarcee Camp, Alberta. A sign of the tough times, the single PPCLI battalion held training sessions on only four occasions during the 20 years between the wars.

The PPCLI was mobilized for active service on September 1, 1939, and with successful recruiting drives in Winnipeg and on Vancouver Island, the Battalion was brought up to full strength by October, under the command of Lieutenant-Colonel W. G. "Shorty" Colquhoun. The regiment sailed from Halifax on December 21, 1939, aboard the *Orama* as part of the 1st Canadian Division.

Soon after its arrival on British soil, the regiment moved to Aldershot, England, the central command post of the British military. Lieutenant-Colonel Colquhoun presented the regiment to the colonel-in-chief herself, Princess Patricia, at Bagshot Park, and on February 10, 1940, she inspected her regiment for the first time in 21 years.

The Patricia's spent the next three years in Britain, mostly engaged in coastal defence and training throughout the country. On July 10, 1943, the 1st Canadian Infantry Division landed in Sicily as part of the 8th Army. The Patricia's were re-introduced to the unpleasantness of warfare at Leonforte, their first World War II battle.

Following the capture of Sicily by the Allies, the regiment landed at Reggio di Calabria, on the tip of Italy's "toe," on September 4, 1943. Benito Mussolini was ousted from power, and Italy's new government signed an armistice with the Allies just a few days later, on September 8.

The Patricia's spent the next two months advancing up the mountainous spine of the Italian peninsula against an embittered German foe. The winter of 1943 saw the regiment fighting battles in Villa Rogatti, "the Gully" and Ortona, winning many individual and regimental honours along the way. During 1944, the Patricia's took part in offensives on the Hitler and Gothic lines, San Fortunato and Rimini, winning several more battle honours that now adorn the regimental colours and cementing their reputation as one of the hardest fighting regiments in Canada. The Patricia's left Italy, bound for North West Europe in March 1945.

By April 1945, the PPCLI was fighting to liberate Holland along with the rest of the 1st Canadian Division, and on April 11, it played a central role in the capture of Apeldoorn. On May 7, two days after Victory in Europe (VE) Day, the Patricia's were the first Allied troops in Amsterdam.

On June 1, 1945, a new battalion of the regiment—later known as the 2nd Battalion, Princess Patricia's Canadian Light Infantry (2 PPCLI)—was authorized to form part of the Canadian Pacific Force in the campaign against Japan. It was subsequently disbanded following the destruction of

Hiroshima and Nagasaki by atomic bombs that caused Japan's surrender on August 15, 1945. The decimated 1st Battalion (1 PPCLI) returned to Winnipeg in October 1945, and was also demobilized.

Just five years later, on August 15, 1950, a new conflict erupted on the Pacific Rim when Chinese and Soviet-backed communist North Korea invaded democratic South Korea, instigating the first United Nations "police action." The Patricia's were reorganized to join the Canadian UN contingent, forming part of the 27th British Commonwealth Brigade. On November 25, 1950, the 2nd Battalion sailed from Seattle on the *Private Joe P. Martinez* bound for Pusan, Korea, where it arrived in December 1950, and on February 6, 1951, became the first Canadian infantry unit to join the war.

On April 22, 1951, the troops of 2 PPCLI fought in one of the most famous Canadian battles outside of the World Wars. The North Koreans had begun a major offensive to recapture Seoul, pitting a huge mass of Chinese People's Liberation Army fighters against the UN Forces in the Kapyong Valley. The forward positions were held by the Patricia's and the 3rd Battalion Royal Australian Regiment, while the heavy gun support was provided by the 72nd U.S. Heavy Tank Regiment's Alpha Company. The Chinese attack concentrated first on the Australian position, then on the Canadian front line. Wave after massive wave of Chinese soldiers crashed upon the allied lines throughout the night of April 22, and by the morning of April 23, the Chinese had infiltrated the brigade position and completely surrounded the Patricia's. The fighting reached a desperate level on April 24, with the tenacious Aussies and Canucks resorting to hand-to-hand combat with bayonet charges.

The Patricia's were only able to receive supplies by airdrop, while the Australians were totally cut off and were forced to retreat later that day. However, the Canadians refused to give up their position and continued to face the overwhelming Chinese forces until their attack finally crumpled. The Canadian's unshakable defence halted the Chinese advance and left the battlefield strewn with over 1000 enemy dead and many more wounded, compared to Canadian losses of 10 killed and 23 wounded, and Australian losses of 31 killed, 59 wounded and 3 captured. Moreover, they prevented the almost certain fall of Seoul into enemy hands, saving the lives of untold numbers of South Koreans and UN troops. For their "extraordinary heroism and outstanding performance of combat duties," they were awarded a U.S. Presidential Unit Citation.

On November 30, 1950, the 3rd Battalion of the regiment was formed, to provide reinforcements for both the 1st and 2nd Battalions during their tours of duty in Korea.

After the Korean War ended in 1953, the Patricia's returned to Canada and entered the *hors de combat* phase of its existence, either fulfilling Canada's NATO obligations or working with the UN on various missions in Cyprus, Israel, the Golan Heights, Egypt, Lebanon, Kuwait, Iraq, the Congo, Vietnam, Central America, Angola, Somalia, Rwanda, Korea and most recently in Croatia and Bosnia.

The UN Protection Force (UNPROFOR) was established in February 1992 to keep the peace in the break-away republics of Croatia and then Bosnia-Herzegovina, both formerly part of Yugoslavia, where Catholic Croats, Orthodox Serbs, and Muslim Bosniaks fought each other for control of their respective enclaves and where the unsavoury term "ethnic cleansing" came into popular usage.

In June 1992, when the Bosnian war began, the Canadian units originally deployed to Croatia were moved south to the area around Bihac, near the Croatian-Bosnian border. Major-General Lewis MacKenzie, a Patricia officer, commanded Sector Sarajevo during the summer of 1992 and presided over the reopening of Sarajevo airport, allowing humanitarian aid to flow into the area. However, the most important accomplishment out of the three years that the Patricia's served with UNPROFOR came during fall of the next year, near the Croatian town of Medak, where the 2nd Battalion fought the largest battle involving Canadian troops since the Korean War.

On September 15, 1993, against heavy opposi-
tion, 250 troops from 2 PPCLI forced the Croatians
to withdraw and stop "cleansing" Serb villages in
an area known as the Medak Pocket in south-
central Croatia. The members of 2 PPCLI, along
with 500 French soldiers, under the command of
Patricia's Lieutenant-Colonel Jim Calvin, moved
between the Serb and Croat front lines and came
under a hail of cannon, mortar and machine-gun
fire from the Croatian side. During that day,
through the night and into the early hours of the
next morning, the Patricia's fought 20 separate
gun battles, eventually forcing the Croats to
retreat.

On the morning of September 16, an armoured
platoon led by Major Dan Drew started towards
a group of Serb villages that the Croatians were
razing. A heavily armed Croatian unit engaged
the platoon, and a pitched gun battle ensued for
90 minutes. The Croatians were finally pushed
back, but 16 bodies were found in the Serb village
of Licki Citluk, where 312 houses and barns—
every single building in the Medak area—had
been burned to the ground.

The battle earned the 2 PPCLI Battle Group its
first-ever UN unit citation. The Canadian government kept the event out of the news until
1996—three years later—ostensibly due to the
"Somalia Affair" that was grabbing headlines at
the time. However, the government did award
Warrant Officer Bill Johnson a Medal of Bravery

for rescuing a French peacekeeper trapped in a minefield during the closing days of the operation, and Lieutenant-Colonel Calvin received the Meritorious Service Cross.

The signing of the Dayton Agreement by warring factions in 1995 began NATO's involvement in the region with its Implementation Force (IFOR), followed by the Stabilization Force (SFOR). The 2 PPCLI Battle Group (the "battle group" designation refers to the logistics soldiers, tanks, engineers and others that are added to a battalion's regular troops to make it "battle ready") served with SFOR in 1997.

The regiment today consists of two mechanized battalions (1 PPCLI and 2 PPCLI) and one light battalion (3 PPCLI), which is also trained for paratrooper capabilities. The 1st and 3rd Battalions are stationed in Edmonton, Alberta, while the 2nd Battalion, formerly of Winnipeg, is now headquartered in Shilo, Manitoba. The regiment participated in the Manitoba Flood Relief operation during the spring of 1997, the Québec and Eastern Ontario ice storm relief operation in January 1998, and since late 2001, all 3500 Patricias have been mobilized for duty in Afghanistan to contribute to the international war against terrorism.

Between February 4 and July 30, 2002, the 3 PPCLI Battle Group was involved in Operations Apollo and Enduring Freedom. This was the first deployment into combat operations by a Canadian Army unit against a declared enemy in five decades. The 3 PPCLI Battle Group was initially responsible for defending the Kandahar airport facility, followed by a stint at Bagram airbase, just outside Kabul. It went on to participate in Operation Harpoon, an air assault in the Shah-i-Kot Valley to find and destroy remnants of Taliban and Al-Qaeda fighters in the nearby mountains, which also involved climbing to elevations of 3000–3600 metres and hunting through caves looking for Al-Qaeda. In May, the Patricia's searched the cave complexes in the Tora Bora Mountains, where Osama bin Laden was reputed to have been hiding.

In March 2002, two teams of Patricia snipers gained recognition while operating independently from the rest of the 3rd Battalion during Operation Anaconda. During the operation, the highly trained snipers killed an estimated 20 enemy fighters, several of them while defending U.S. troops who were under fire during one particularly intense engagement. An American battalion was sustaining mortar fire from suspected Taliban and Al-Qaeda fighters while moving down a ridge in the Shah-i-Kot Valley. Even though the 3rd Battalion also became the target of enemy artillery, the snipers' steady hands never wavered, and they neutralized several enemy positions from as far away as two kilometres, allowing the Americans to continue towards their final objective. For their skills and the many lives they no doubt saved, all of the Patricia's snipers were awarded U.S. Bronze Stars.

In sombre contrast to that great achievement is the event that took place in the early hours of April 18, 2002—the "friendly fire" incident in Tarnac Puhl, about 14 kilometres from Kandahar. About 100 paratroopers of 3 PPCLI's Alpha Company were engaged in nighttime live fire training, when an American F-16 pilot, thinking the enemy was firing him on, dropped a laser-guided 225-kilo-gram bomb on their position. Four Patricias were killed instantly and eight wounded, two critically. Their deaths—the first in combat against a declared foe since the Korean War—put the country in mourning for losing four of its sons in such a tragic and senseless way. However, among their brothers-in-arms, it gave their contribution to the war that much more meaning.

In the words of one soldier: "It made everyone work all that much harder and take their jobs that much more seriously, because we wanted to make sure that we didn't let these guys down."

Notes on Sources

Berton, Pierre. *The Invasion of Canada*. Toronto: McLelland and Stewart Ltd., 1980.

Berton, Pierre. *Flames Across the Border*. Toronto: McClelland and Stewart Ltd., 1981.

Bishop, William Arthur. *The Courage of the Early Morning: A Son's Biography of a Famous Father*. Toronto: McClelland and Stewart Ltd., 1965.

Casgrain, Abbé H.R. *Wolfe and Montcalm*. Toronto: University of Toronto Press, 1964.

Edgar, Lady. *General Brock*. Toronto: Morang & Co., Ltd., 1904.

Edmunds, R. David. *Tecumseh and the Quest for Indian Leadership*: Toronto: Little, Brown and Co., Ltd., 1984.

James, Melbourne. *Canada Heirloom Series, Volume VI Visionaries: Canadian Triumphs*. Toronto: Heirloom Publishing Inc., 1998.

McKenzie, Ruth. *Laura Secord: The Lady and the Legend*. Toronto: McClelland and Stewart Ltd., 1971.

Off, Carol. *The Lion the Fox and the Eagle: A Story of Generals and Justice in Yugoslavia and Rwanda*. Toronto: Random House Canada, 2000.

Parkham, Francis. *Montcalm and Wolfe*. Toronto: Ryerson Press, 1964.

Speaight, Robert. *Vanier: Soldier, Diplomat and Governor General*. Toronto: Collins, 1970.

Urquhart, Hugh M. *Arthur Currie: The Biography of a Great Canadian*. Toronto: J.M. Dent & Sons Ltd., 1950.